LITERARY/CULTURAL THEORY

PSYCHO ANALYTIC THEORY AND CRITICISM

Literary/Cultural Theory provides concise and lucid introductions to a range of key concepts and theorists in contemporary literary and cultural theory. Original and contemporary in presentation, and eschewing jargon, each book in the series presents students of humanities and social sciences exhaustive overviews of theories and theorists, while also introducing them to the mechanics of reading literary/cultural texts using critical tools. Each book also carries glossaries of key terms and ideas, and pointers for further reading and research. Written by scholar-teachers who have taught critical theory for years, and vetted by some of the foremost experts in the field, the series Literary/Cultural Theory is indispensable to students and teachers.

Also in the series

Feminisms
Marxist Literary and Cultural Theory
Ecocriticism
Queer Studies
Dalit Literature and Criticism
Postcolonialism Now
Frantz Fanon
Jacques Lacan
Periyar
Edward Said
Mikhail Bakhtin
Popular Culture
Diaspora Theory and Transnationalism
Postsecular Theory
Nations and Nationalisms
Life Writing
Subaltern Studies
Posthumanism
Deconstruction and Poststructuralism

LITERARY/CULTURAL THEORY

PSYCHO ANALYTIC THEORY AND CRITICISM

By way of an Introduction to the Writings of Sigmund Freud

ANDREW SLADE
University of Dayton, Ohio

Orient BlackSwan

PSYCHOANALYTIC THEORY AND CRITICISM

ORIENT BLACKSWAN PRIVATE LIMITED

Registered Office
3-6-752 Himayatnagar, Hyderabad 500 029, Telangana, India
e-mail: centraloffice@orientblackswan.com

Other Offices
Bengaluru, Chennai, Guwahati, Hyderabad,
Kolkata, Mumbai, New Delhi, Noida, Patna

First published 2016
Reprinted 2017, 2020, 2025

ISBN 978 81 250 6072 7

Typeset in Aldine 401 BT 10.5/13 *by*
Mindshine Book House
Hyderabad 500 060

040160

Printed at
B.B. Press, Tronica City, Ghaziabad, UP 201 103

Published by
Orient Blackswan Private Limited
3-6-752 Himayatnagar, Hyderabad 500 029, Telangana, India
e-mail: info@orientblackswan.com

Contents

Preface

I have designed this book to keep with the mission of the series, *Literary/Cultural Theory*, as books to help students to begin and deepen their studies of literature and theory. The book, then, has a didactic purpose, though I hope to cling lightly to that so as to help students learn the basic moves of psychoanalytic theory and criticism as they have developed in the last hundred years, and as they have been put to use in literary and cultural studies. It is difficult to imagine literary and cultural studies today without some encounter with Freud and Freudian theory. Yet, far too often the references to psychoanalysis are taken as the basis of criticism and theory as if psychoanalysis has always been around as a set of tools to be picked up or discarded, to be accepted dogmatically or rejected wholesale. Psychoanalysis has a history and, like the rest of history, it is possible to imagine and to know a world without it – yet that is not our world. For us in the globalised twenty-first century, psychoanalysis has always been part of our present even if only as a joke about a slip of the tongue or about whether a cigar is, in fact, sometimes just a cigar or if, as a simplified and dogmatic psychoanalysis would have it, a cigar is always a penis.

I assume a beginner's level of knowledge of Freud and Freudian theory – you may have heard of psychoanalysis, perhaps been to see a counsellor or psychotherapist, or perhaps only heard a mention of any of these. Regardless, you are likely to have some familiarity with Freud's ideas if only in a popular and diluted form. Indeed, few thinkers' ideas have so permeated global intellectual and cultural flows as have Freud's. Freudian ideas are almost everywhere. Reading this book, you will come to recognise them when you see them, and perhaps, look beyond the diluted and simplified form that they take in mass culture and learn to question and to understand how their more technical use and formulation can help us understand our experiences in the early twenty-first century and importantly, understand and make some sense of literary and cultural texts from a variety of places, periods, languages and cultures.

In this book I focus on Freud's texts. For the most part, I focus my attention on texts that are widely considered to be of major importance in the elaboration of psychoanalytic theory and in the development of psychoanalytic literary theory. Psychoanalytic literary criticism is an interdisciplinary approach to literature and culture and so, as students begin to engage with psychoanalysis they will have to engage with Freud's texts even as they build the skill and habits of the best readers of literary texts. I begin the book with those texts to suggest the core of the discipline at the same time as I remind us all that those texts are just the beginning. They remain the place to start even as over a century beyond the original publication of many of these texts, considerable work by other psychoanalysts and literary and cultural theorists have refined and developed their themes and arguments. This book is the beginning and though I do my best to account for some of that later work, I do that through the choice of my presentation and argument rather than through the elaboration of a specific history of psychoanalytic theory and criticism. The purpose of the book is to lay the groundwork for further questions and further work. After reading it, you should be prepared for that work.

Andrew Slade

Chapter One

Sigmund Freud and the Itinerary of Psychoanalysis

Psychoanalysis is a revolutionary theory of the mind, of feeling and of behaviour. It evolved over time in Vienna, Austria, in the late nineteenth century, through the curiosity and ambition of Sigmund Freud (1856–1939) and his interlocutors from around the world who were drawn to his work. This book is an introduction to psychoanalysis and psychoanalytic literary theory by way of an introduction to the work of Sigmund Freud. Any introduction to Freud's theories will bring us into contact with Freud's literary examples. Freud read widely in the history of literature and cultures and was a man of considerable curiosity. When he looked for examples that his readers might be familiar with, he turned to many famous literary characters. Psychoanalytic theory, from its beginning, is already literary.

Freud was the first and the most beloved son of Jakob Freud and Amalia Freud (*née* Nathansohn), Prussian Jews who sought the best education for their son. He was born in 1856 in Silesia, in what is today the Czech Republic. Privileged among his brothers and sisters, Freud received an enviable education and hoped to find a career in research in neurology. He was an excellent student and diligent at his work. When his academic career was cut short due almost entirely to Austrian anti-Semitism, he became a clinician, whereas he had desired, above all, to be a researcher and professor.

Freud lived and worked in Vienna, Austria, in the late nineteenth century and through the first thirty-eight years of the twentieth. He fled to London in 1938 when the Nazi invasion of Austria made it clear that Jews were not safe there. In the years from his first psychoanalytic publications in the 1890s to the first major work of psychoanalytic theory, *The Interpretation of Dreams* (1900), Freud worked in his clinic to establish psychoanalysis as a path of treatment and research into the workings of the human mind. It was not long until others began to develop Freud's ideas in treatment and research. In fewer than twenty years, there was already an established network of psychoanalysts practising, writing and sharing their research. Writers and artists picked up Freudian themes and put them to use in their creative works. Freud and other analysts were quick to pick up on that interest to venture into the analysis of individual works of art and literature as well as works about individual artists and writers. The American poet H. D. (Hilda Doolitle, 1886–1961) sought treatment with Freud and then published her account of that treatment as *Tribute to Freud* (1956) though some portions of the book had appeared earlier than that in 1944. In 1924, André Breton praised Freud in *The Manifestoes of Surrealism* for bringing his 'critical faculties to bear upon the dream' (10). The avant-garde in art and literature engaged with Freud's understanding of dreams and dream processes in their own creative processes. In painting, literature and in cinema, Freud's discoveries of the unconscious and dream processes stoked the imaginations of artists and writers and provided, for many of them, a theoretical basis for their artistic practices.

Psychoanalysis has developed substantially since Freud worked and wrote. Psychoanalytic societies and institutes have been established all over the world and psychoanalysts have seen patients, written case histories, and developed theory and clinical techniques for their practices that serve their societies. Today, the International Psychoanalytic Association lists forty-seven affiliates in Europe, North America, Latin America and Asia. Though the majority of affiliated societies remain in the West, there are long-standing Psychoanalytic Associations worldwide.

This introduction to psychoanalytic theory and criticism will focus on the foundational concepts in Freudian theory because even as psychoanalysis has developed and changed, most analysts adhere to Freud's basic insights. In an interview with Ramin Jahanbegloo, the eminent Indian psychoanalyst, Sudhir Kakar says,

> I completely subscribe to his [Freud's] basic assumptions, such as the importance of the unconscious part of the mind in our thought, behavior, and action, the vital significance of early childhood experiences for later life, the importance of Eros in human motivation, the dynamic interplay, including conflict between the conscious and unconscious parts of the mind. (Jahanbegloo 30)

Kakar objects to certain formulations of Freud's thought and endorses the fundamentals of Freud's theory of the mind. Kakar's objections to Freud's arguments and emphases do not imply the wholesale rejection of the psychoanalytic enterprise in developing a theory of the mind and an effective therapeutic intervention, any more than a general agreement with the fundamental claims of the theory implies wholesale and entire endorsement. These key terms – unconscious, repression, wish fulfilment and others – comprise the key vocabulary of psychoanalytic theory. As with any cohesive body of theory and practice, psychoanalysis has changed and developed since Freud's time. Other analysts have disagreed with Freud, sometimes on significant issues, and still the emphasis on the unconscious, on dreams, on the foundational claims that Freud described in his psychoanalytic work remain the foundation of psychoanalytic theory. There have been periods of more and less stringent dogmatism where conformity in psychoanalysis was emphasised over new developments in theory and practice. There have been different national trends and emphases that have developed over time due to the interventions of different analysts and in response to the working conditions – social and institutional – of different nations. The beginner student of psychoanalytic theory and criticism ought to recognise that, by now, psychoanalysis has developed around the globe from the ground of Freud's works, but has been guided by many different theorists and authors who have intervened in psychoanalysis for their local needs and ends.

The basic assumptions of Freudian thought that Kakar refers to form the core of the itinerary of this book that aims to introduce students to these fundamental psychoanalytic insights, to how those insights have affected literary criticism and theory, and to how psychoanalytic knowledge and experience influence reading and writing about literature. Dreams and the Unconscious, the importance of childhood and play, the struggle between Eros and Thanatos, of life and love and death, the mistakes of everyday life, those wishes and fantasies that attract and frighten us – these are the themes and domains of psychoanalysis as much as they are of literature. These are the areas of reading, and of life, that psychoanalytic criticism and theory aim to understand and to question.

A VERY BRIEF HISTORY OF PSYCHOANALYSIS IN FREUD'S WRITINGS

Freud's psychoanalytic writing spans twenty-four volumes in *The Standard Edition of the Complete Psychological Works of Sigmund Freud*, published at the Hogarth Press under the general editorship of James Strachey, between 1953 and 1974. Scholars refer to this as the *Standard Edition* (SE) and all of the citations in this book refer to the *Standard Edition*. Volume 1 of the *Standard Edition* collects Freud's work from 1886 to 1899 and includes his early work on hypnotism. Freud had long been interested in psychiatric work and neurology. He aspired to be a researcher, but his ethnic identity as a Jew in Austria kept him from realising those ambitions. He travelled to Paris and studied under Jean-Martin Charcot (1825–93). There Freud saw the effects of hypnosis in the treatment of people who suffered from hysteria. Hysteria is a psychological disturbance that affects many areas of a person's life and it manifests in a variety of physical symptoms that do not have clear physiological causes. For example, something as minor as a cough that will not go away, or a paralysis of the arm for which there is no apparent cause, or the loss of speech without a clear physical cause. Charcot was a professor at the famous Parisian Hospital known as the Salpêtrière and he had been treating neurological disorders with hypnosis. These were hysterical symptoms that psychoanalysis, among other ailments, sought to treat. Prior to the development of psychoanalytic methods, doctors treated hysteria with hypnotism and hypnotic suggestions, and Freud learned from them.

Freud's writing was wide ranging. He wrote technical works on psychoanalytic theory and practice to advance psychoanalytic knowledge for other analysts, and he also wrote for a more general, erudite audience. These books and essays take a variety of forms: from reports on specialised topics of techniques and applications of psychoanalytic ideas, to problems from other disciplines, papers on metapsychology, case studies and speculations on cultural issues. As a body of writing in its own right, Freud's corpus is expansive in its scope and ambitious in its execution.

Hysteria and the Method of the 'Talking Cure'

Psychoanalysis is a theoretical and practical discipline that was born from the clinic but not restricted to it. Freud developed psychoanalysis in the beginning of the twentieth century as a method of treating nervous disorders in his patients. Freud was trained as a neurologist and aspired to a career in research. As a Jew in the anti-Semitic context of Victorian Austria, his academic ambitions were closed to him though he had the intellect, the talent and the ambition to succeed. When it became clear to him that he would not have an academic research career, he began clinical work. In the 1880s, Freud worked in the clinic with Josef Breuer (1842–1925), a Viennese clinician, where he treated hysterics with hypnosis, and began to develop with Breuer, what they called the 'cathartic method' and which the famous patient Anna O. called, 'the talking cure'. The purpose of the treatment was to purge the mind of thoughts and convictions that bound the patient to her suffering. The cure became known, famously, as the 'talking cure' because the method that brought about relief from symptoms involved talking about the internal conflicts and history that had brought the patient to the clinic to begin with. Talk can cure – this is the basic conviction of the cathartic method. The talk was thought to cure based on the patient's ability to recognise internal conflict and to see and understand that the conflict could be overcome if she were to think and act differently in relation to the conflict. Freud thought, initially, that the cure to hysteria might be as simple as helping the patient to see her conflicts.

The aim of the talking cure was to achieve the discharge of intellectual and psychical energy; and the discharge of energy allowed the patient to live his or her life without the persistence of the symptoms. The cathartic method was limited, in Freud's view, and its successes hard to come by. In successful treatment, he witnessed the alleviation of symptoms together with a revision of the structure that gave rise to them through a reordering of psychical material from the patient's life that had been locked way, nearly forgotten, but recalled, revisited and reworked in treatment by talking. Psychoanalysis, as it came to be called by Freud, was the method of accomplishing this work and it involved the patient talking and the doctor listening.

The *Studies* are made up of descriptions of hysterical symptoms, case histories, and theoretical remarks on the psychology of hysteria and its treatment. Hysterical symptoms include paralysis that is not explained by physiological causes, an inability to speak, epileptic style fits or fainting. There is no clear physical reason for any of the symptoms. The source of hysterical symptoms was not well-known when Freud and Breuer practised. The case studies and treatments of hysterics that they conducted lead them to believe that memory played a significant role in hysterical symptoms. 'Hysterics,' they wrote, 'suffer mainly from reminiscences' (SE II 7). Hysterical memory is not made up of common memories that fade as time passes. 'The memories which have become the determinants of hysterical phenomena persist for a long time with astonishing freshness and with the whole of their affective colouring' (SE II 9). Hysterical memory differs from ordinary memory in its intensity of emotional appeal. In hysterical memory, the object of the memory appears again as if it were present rather than as a moment of one past moment. In this sense, the hysteric suffers from their memory.

The point of the treatment that Freud utilised was to remove hysterical symptoms by means of catharsis or purgation of the remembered material that was at the source of the patient's suffering. The idea was that by talking through the memory and bringing the patient to understand the memory as a memory in the past rather than a present threat, the patient could find some relief from the symptom. Freud closes the theoretical section of the *Studies* with the following remark:

> When I have promised my patients help or improvement by means of a cathartic treatment I have often been faced by this objection: "Why, you tell me yourself that my illness is probably connected with my circumstances and the events of my life. You cannot alter these in any way. How do you propose to help me then?" And I have been able to make this reply: "No doubt fate would find it easier that I do to relieve you of your illness. But you will be able to convince your self that much will be gained if we succeed in transforming your hysterical misery into common unhappiness. With a mental life that has been restored to health you will be better armed against that unhappiness." (SE II 305).

This passage holds much of what comes to be called Freud's pessimism about human life. The aim of his treatment is not to make people happy who are unhappy. In fact, over the course of his life and work, Freud becomes increasingly sceptical about human happiness. We do not become happy, but we can live with our unhappiness in a more fruitful and less miserable way, with the events and circumstances of our lives as they are rather than as we wish them to be. This sceptical thesis would be given considerable thought in his later work, *Civilisation and Its Discontents*.

Studies on Hysteria (SE II) was published in 1895 and is often recognised as a transitional work from the cathartic method of treating hysteria to the nascent or emerging theoretical and clinical work of psychoanalysis. Looking back over the development of psychoanalysis, we might say that *Studies on Hysteria* presents an emergent version of psychoanalysis and represents the experience with hysteria in the clinic that brings Freud to psychoanalysis and to the first major intervention in psychoanalytic theory, *The Interpretation of Dreams*, a work that remains foundational today. A basic insight of psychoanalysis is that human thought, feeling, and behaviour do not belong fully to our conscious mind. Parts of our experience exceed our ability to control them consciously and these unconscious thoughts, feelings and behaviours become the focus of psychoanalytic thought; and *The Interpretation of Dreams* is a major step in Freud's articulation of the unconscious processes of the mind. He describes these processes by understanding and interpreting dreams.

Dreams and Interpretation

In *The Interpretation of Dreams*, Freud describes the dream as the effect of the Unconscious and its singular activity – wishing. What the Unconscious cannot have in waking life, the mind wishes for in sleep. Human life is a life of disappointments. Often, we do not get what we want during our days. At night, the unconscious is able to satisfy our wishes in dreams. Freud regarded *The Interpretation of Dreams* as one of his most significant works and it appeared in several editions during his life. It sold slowly at first, though as psychoanalysis took root across Europe and the rest of the world, it was a text that he continued to edit, augment and refine. It is his first major work that is 'metapsychological' in orientation. That is, it describes concrete mental phenomena and offers a theoretical account of those phenomena beyond mere description. The metapsychology that Freud describes in *The Interpretation of Dreams* forms the substantial base of psychoanalysis and he will continue to add to the theory during his life, in later publications.

As Freud's first major work in psychoanalytic metapsychology, the book is a touchstone of psychoanalytic theory as well as a controversial classic of intellectual and scholarly achievement. When it appeared at the beginning of the twentieth century, it gave rise to a swell of criticism and curiosity. The book itself is a compendium of anecdotes and insights, of analysis and criticism that unfolds page after page and finds its apogee in the final chapters where Freud takes up a sustained theoretical discussion of the processes of dreaming.

Though dense and sometimes obscure, this foundational volume in psychoanalytic theory systematically presents the basis of Freud's newly-born discipline. The book was published in late 1899, but Freud wanted it to be dated for the new century and so it bears the date 1900. It was not particularly well-received in the beginning, though it would go through multiple editions as Freud's ideas spread. The 'dream book', as Freud called it, stands as one of the most significant texts of psychoanalysis, but it is also among the most significant and widely influential books of the twentieth century. Key psychoanalytic terms find their first articulation in this book. Ideas like the dream work, censorship, condensation and displacement, the pleasure principle, etc., will become the groundwork for the psychoanalytic account of mental life. These terms, which I will take up in detail below, will also be taken up in literary and cultural criticism. The major Freudian discovery is the notion that much of human mental life is unconscious and that the unconscious is a dynamic, primary, mental process that seeks its satisfactions through wishing.

The Interpretation of Dreams is a significant contribution to psychoanalytic metapsychology. Metapsychology is the overall theoretical interpretation of human psychic life from infancy, through childhood and adolescence, through adulthood and old age. It is a comprehensive account of human mental life and psychoanalytical metapsychology focuses on unconscious mental processes as much as it does on conscious ones. Contemporary psychology lacks a metapsychology and focuses its disciplinary attention to those phenomena that are visible, observable, repeatable and testable in a laboratory environment. At the time of Freud's writing, psychology was emerging as a scientific discipline. Psychoanalysis retained the need for a theoretical account of human mental life while what becomes scientific psychology (as taught in modern universities) treats metapsychology with scepticism and instead invests its authority in largely statistical methods and instruments and tests that produce statistical data. Psychoanalytic metapsychology seeks to account for the range of human psychic life by foundational concepts; in particular, the unconscious.

One of the strengths of psychoanalytic theory is that it maps onto human experience. It is derived from the clinical encounter with people who were suffering but whose suffering had no clear causes. Freud's inquiry into the basic functioning of human mental life aimed to account for this fundamental opacity of the human mind. From observations of neurotics and children Freud derived considerable knowledge about unconscious processes that apply not only to neurotics, but to all of human mental life. In this book, Freud describes the function of dreaming and its relation to the unconscious. In our infancy, wishing accomplishes our satisfaction in relation to our basic helplessness. The human infant is fundamentally helpless. It requires significant care by an other – often, though not exclusively, the mother provides that care. When an infant cries, it expresses its dissatisfaction and its mother responds to the cry and satisfies the dissatisfaction. Infantile helplessness sustains and prolongs the time before the infant encounters reality. In early infancy, the infant cannot be let alone for any significant length of time. The encounter with reality is an encounter with dissatisfaction and the mental response to that dissatisfaction, which is born of helplessness and the delay in the mother's attention to our satisfactions, produces an hallucinatory response. If we cannot get what we want, when we want it, we will take another object that approximates the desired object. If we cannot have the approximation, the unconscious can be satisfied by a hallucination. The theory of dreams accounts for the way in which dissatisfaction can be stayed by a hallucination.

Psychoanalytic criticism begins with dreams and desires that circulate from the unconscious. Dreams are particular to each of us and find their materials in our day's experiences and from the social and cultural facts of our lives. Psychoanalysis is not universal in the sense that it demands dogmatism, but it is universal in the insistence upon the structure of the unconscious as a dynamic, wishing machine. Psychoanalytic criticism and theory migrate across cultures and languages in ways that people might, and in the ways that literature does. Psychoanalytic criticism approaches literature as a dynamic expression of human desire. Literature provides psychoanalysis with a wealth of exemplars and models just as psychoanalysis supplies literature with a systematic way of linking works of imagination to theory and practice.

The structures of the unconscious and unconscious processes can be generalised across culture and language, but the contents of those processes are quite contingent on both culture and language. In this claim, I depart from Freud whose thought was bound to a particular moment of Viennese modernity. For Freud, there was no question that his discoveries were universalisable. As I will discuss at length below, there is no reason to claim that the specific cultural references that are foundational to psychoanalysis – the importance of Hamlet or Oedipus being the most obvious – limit the sway of psychoanalysis to what is called the 'western world'. From a metapsychological point of view, the unconscious is a wishing machine. At the core of any psychoanalytic theory there is an anthropological claim: that is, a claim about the basic nature of human beings. The primary condition of the human being is frailty, vulnerability, helpless in its beginnings. This original helplessness initiates the process of wishing. The primary way beyond helplessness is wishing; the first way out of the panic that helplessness induces is wishing.

The unconscious tries to overcome the frailty of human existence and its deprivations through wishing; yet, that wishing can likewise become, through the secondary process of repression, a source of immense pain and suffering. In the psychoanalytical sense, neurosis is the effect of too much escape from a reality that presses too closely to us, that cuts us too much to the quick, that intrudes in the ease and comfort we desire for our days and our nights. The world intrudes into our sense of safety and well-being, and we will seek ways that we do not have. Neurosis can become the solution to this 'reality problem' – the problem that we cannot always and everywhere have our pains and needs relieved. We cannot avoid helplessness and deprivations as once we were able to, in infancy.

Infantile helplessness persists over the course of our lives as one of the major facts of unconscious life. The unconscious knows no time; that is, in the unconscious, the past is as present as if it were unfolding at this very moment. The 'now' is an extension of all prior moments that abide unconsciously as if without sequence – for indeed, to be timeless will have meant to be without sequence; hence, the dynamism of the unconscious is also a spatial dynamism in which different moments in conscious time – that is, in time as we experience it in waking life – can be mapped over sequences that appear out of order. That the unconscious is without time also means that in the unconscious, the sequential logic of time – that one moment passes another – does not hold. For the unconscious, time is irrelevant. The unconscious is the dynamic repository of wishes that are expressed as the response to real or imagined deprivations. Real deprivations can be overcome, at least in an infantile way, through unconscious processes of fantasy, dream formation and symptom formation. Neurosis is not a problem but a problem that has formed as the solution to another problem, as Paul Verhaeghe has suggested, in his re-reading of the Oedipus Complex in *New Studies of Old Villains*. Verhaeghe claims that there is nothing essential to the story of Oedipus in psychoanalysis – it is contingent on cultural location that Oedipus becomes the primary story in Freud's theory. The generalisable structure is that the neurotic response to problems itself becomes a problem. Neurosis is the mental defence against a reality that is either too dangerous to encounter directly or a psychological response to an imagined deprivation or the return of repressed material into daily life.

Dreams and fantasies, symptoms and daydreams, get us what we cannot have in daily life – these are the mechanisms that our mental and psychical apparatus uses to shield us from the pains of deprivation and the psychological pains of imagined deprivations. Dreams allow us to have what we cannot have; they salve our real and imagined wounds. Dreams correct our reality. They give in our sleep what we cannot have while awake.

While the unconscious wishes and seeks its satisfactions, the demands of reality on us militate against clear and complete satisfaction. In the simplest terms, some of our wishes are impossible to actualise. Rather than endure the pain of deprivation, the process of repression intervenes on our wishes and they are renounced for us by us. Repression is a process by which our minds protect us from satisfying wishes and desires that would get us punished either in reality (by our mother or father or some other authority) or, having internalised the threat of punishment, imagining the punishment.

Repression is a secondary process that aligns with the demands of waking life and the demands of reality to conceal our most coveted wishes. Repression protects us from the dangerous wishes of the unconscious in the context of our daily lives and the demands of our social and cultural reality. Even while asleep, there is repression at work through dream censorship – a mechanism that works to keep dangerous wishes from appearing too clearly. The unconscious uses condensation and displacement to conceal the wish from dream censorship. Censorship is weaker than repression, though it belongs to the same secondary processes. The interpretation of a dream is generated by the dreamer's associations with the images of the dream and his or her unfolding narrative about the dream and its images in telling the dream to the analyst.

Dream interpretation gives us some key concepts in psychoanalysis. It brings out the fact that the unconscious is a primary process of mental life. The unconscious is the mechanism that generates dreams. Our dreams are not non-sense, though they do require interpretation if we are to understand them psychoanalytically. All dreams are wish fulfilments. Even anxiety dreams are wish fulfilments. All dreams are composed of a manifest content – the conscious representation of the dream – and the manifest content conceals a latent dream thought. The latent dream thought is the wish that motivates the dream; it is the wish at the core of the dream. Dreams are constructed dynamically through the processes of condensation and displacement. The latent dream thought is often too charged to be acceptable to conscious thought without being disguised. The dream process will displace those charged thoughts from one object and substitute it with another, less charged object. In condensation, the charged latent thought is combined with other objects to make a composite that, on its own, is benign. The task of interpreting dreams then is to unravel the latent dream thought from the manifest content of the dream by tracking the work of the condensation or displacement of the dream thoughts into the manifest content of the dream. The analyst listens to the narrative of the dream, and the associations that the dreamer has to the images, and looks for gaps where repression has allowed the latent dream thought to come into the dreamer's discourse. By following dreams, the analyst can find the unconscious thinking at the core of the dreamer's life and experience – at least at that moment. The method of dream interpretation becomes a model for psychoanalytic criticism of literature and culture. The psychoanalytic critic, then, can leverage the theory and methods of dream interpretation in the analysis of literature and culture. We will return to this task below.

Everyday Life and Neurotic Parallels

In *The Psychopathology of Everyday Life* (SE VI, 1901), Freud looks to everyday experiences to explain his theory of human mental functioning. All of psychoanalysis claims that the difference between a sick person and a normal person – between a neurotic and a normal, non-neurotic person – is a difference of degree or quantity and not quality. That is, the neurotic is not fundamentally and qualitatively different from the normal people we encounter in everyday life. As the editorial note of the *Standard Edition* puts it, the mistakes and errors Freud describes in the book 'enabled him to extend to normal mental life the discoveries he had first made in connection with neuroses' (SE VI xii). Freud argues his thesis by referring to evidence from daily lives of non-neurotics and compares those experiences to the clinical evidence he has amassed in his practice. There are certain behaviours that neurotics and non-neurotics share. Everyone seems to make mistakes in identity or attribution even when what the mistake is about is something that we are completely intimate with. We might call someone by the wrong name; we might forget a name. We forget complete sets of words and we have slips of the tongue; we misread text and we make slips in writing. These errors – 'parapraxes' in the language of the *Standard Edition* – suggest that the difference between the neurotic and the non-neurotic is a matter of quantity or intensity. Parapraxes are not likely to cause anyone considerable distress in their lives. Most of us can make a mistake and move along; neurotic symptoms, however, become the mechanism that the neurotic uses to engage with the world and preserve his or her satisfaction. Freud continually expanded these examples in *The Psychopathology of Everyday Life*.

The book reads as a compendium of mistakes – Freud's own mistakes and mistakes he has found in print or in the course of his experience. His conclusion extends his belief that the difference between the sick and the healthy individual is a matter of intensity and not of quality. He writes, 'One thing which the severest and the mildest cases all have in common, and which is equally found in parapraxes [errors] and chance actions: *the phenomena can be traced back to incompletely suppressed psychical material, which, although pushed away by consciousness, has nevertheless not been robbed of all capacity for expressing itself*' (SE VI 279, emphasis added). Just as dreams are comprised of disguised psychical material, thoughts and wishes that are too charged to be accepted in consciousness, errors of waking life are the disguised expressions of material that repression tries to keep from consciousness, but which escapes nonetheless. Freud continues to apply his ideas to the waking life of ordinary experience because he believes that 'psychoneurotic symptoms, and especially the psychical formations of hysteria and obsessional neurosis, repeat in their mechanism all the essential features of this mode of working [that is, the mistakes of daily life]' (SE VI 278).

The Psychopathology of Everyday Life illustrates a method of close textual reading that rivals scholarly reading of literary texts. Frued's method of expanding the book creates a catalogue of errors and slips, along with their interpretations. Freud and Freudian interpretation, as we will see below in the analysis of the 'Dream of Irma's Injection' from *The Interpretation of Dreams*, pay acute attention to the specific, linguistic formulation of the objects that become subject to such close reading. Like literary analysis where the critic must leverage what he or she knows about language in the service of analysis, psychoanalysis uses the language in which dreams and symptoms are articulated to arrive at their significance. Just as the literary critic analyses the text as well as its history and context, the analyst looks at the whole picture of the symptoms and experiences of the analysand, a person undergoing psychoanalysis. This does not mean that the psychoanalytic critic tries to treat the text as if it were a person, but that the articulations of the text are treated as if it were the case that the literary text conceals a more fundamental significance that an analytic reading can reveal.

The Psychoanalytic Theory of Sexuality

Psychoanalysis is most famous, perhaps, in its caricatured form, as an obsession with sex and sexuality. Everyone seems to believe, in advance, that Freudians are obsessed with sex and if you happen to see a psychoanalyst, he or she will probably be interested in hearing about your relationship with your mother and how you are obsessed with desire for her! In fact, the psychoanalytic account of sexuality and sexual development is tied more intimately to psychosexual development than it is to any theory of sexual practice. Sexuality in psychoanalysis bears more on the thoughts and feelings that circulate around particular sites of the body – the so-called erogenous zones – than it does on sexual practice. Indeed, sexual practice comprises a much more narrow field of experience than the affective and cognitive dimensions of sexual life, though the aberrations in sexual life also comprise a significant element of the theory. The theory of sexuality in psychoanalysis is more properly thought of as 'psychosexuality' or the mental life of sex.

The *Three Essays on the Theory of Sexuality* (1905) sketch the basic structure of human development from a psychoanalytic point of view. The essays begin with 'aberrations' of sexual life – what were called 'perversions' and are now called 'paraphilias' in the *Diagnostic and Statistical Manual of the American Psychiatric Association* and in the *International Classification of Diseases.* Both of these diagnostic manuals give an account of aberrational sexual practices as deviant from the norms of human sexual expression and contrary to certain moral and legal norms, especially in regards to sex with children and animals. The second essay is about infantile sexuality and the third deals with the developments of puberty. In these essays, Freud introduces and develops the notion that human beings are sexual beings from infancy and that sexuality is not a late acquired trait.

The first essay on sexual aberrations introduces important psychoanalytic vocabulary – in particular, the notions of libido, sexual object and sexual aim. Libido is the reservoir of sexual appetite or 'hunger' (SE VII 135). Libido is sexual energy. Sexual energy is invested into particular sexual objects or the person who is desired. The sexual aim is the act sought in the sexual drive. Sexuality is libido energy that is invested in an object for a particular aim. Freud treats the aberrations of sexual life as deviations from the norms regarding the object and the aim that libido energy takes.

In the first essay, Freud is concerned with the ways in which sexual life is expressed in relation to the objects and aims of sexual satisfaction. He discusses deviations of objects first, then deviations of the sexual aim, and then perversions. We shall pass over the details of Freud's discussion of the deviations with respect to objects. Freud's discussion of the objects of the sexual drive is rooted in the conventions of his history and in the development of sexual mores in that particular moment. Freud describes the mores of his moment and the ways in which they deviate from the norms of that history. Same-sex desire plays different roles in different places and it has different meanings according to its location in cultures and history. In Freud's Vienna, same-sex desire is a deviation from the normal or the statistically common sexual object. The deviation is not necessarily a normative, ethical claim against same-sex desire. However, in the case of the deviation from the normal object of desire towards children or animals, the deviation is both statistically and ethically beyond the norm. When Freud talks about the normal sexual objects of the sexual drive, he leans on the conventions of his location. Psychoanalysis has been challenged on the premise that it takes a cultural practice and preference as a normative ideal. The *Three Essays* run this risk even as Freud tries to remain as descriptive as possible in his approach to sexuality. Sexual deviation is determined according to local and historical norms.

Freud understands the aim of the sexual act to be intercourse: 'The normal sexual aim is regarded as being the union of the genitals in the act known as copulation, which leads to a release of the sexual tension and a temporary excitation of the sexual instinct – a satisfaction analogous to the sating of hunger' (SE VII 149). This is the conventional view of the sexual aim. Deviations in the sexual aim open up the possibility of sexuality shifting from its conventional aim, to other aims entirely. The deviation of the sexual aim away from the unification of the genitals in intercourse opens a path to perversions: 'Perversions are sexual activities which either (a) extend, in an anatomical sense, beyond regions of the body that are designed for sexual union, or (b) linger over the intermediate relations to the sexual object which should normally be traversed rapidly on the path towards the final sexual aim' (SE VII 150).

Perversions are deviations with regard to the sexual aim and involve the sexual overvaluation of particular parts of the body other than the genitals or a focus on another part of the body that is normally part of the sexual aim but not the genitals. Freud's examples include the sexual interest in the anus and the mouth. In certain cases, a person will stall his or her sexual desire to remain with a component part of the sexual aim. In normal sexuality, some lingering over the body of the sexual object is expected as part of the 'path' (in Freud's words) to the sexual aim. A certain kind of perversion, then, is part of normal sexuality. This sort of perversion is integral to human sexuality in the sense that human sexual expression includes considerably more than the unification of the genitals in intercourse.

However, there are risks in normal sexuality. Perversion results when the detours on the path to the aim of the sexual drive become fixed at points before the full expression of genital union. Most common sexual practices share elements of perversion. Normal sexuality is different from perverse sexuality in its exclusivity and its fixation (SE VII 161). Normal sexuality has a degree of fluidity and openness in the manner in which partners achieve the sexual aim. Literary examples abound in various traditions. The attractive force of a sleeve, for example, in the European courtly love tradition can begin an entire adventure of desire. In the great Tamil epic of Iḷaṅko Aṭikaḷ, *The Cilappatikāram,* an anklet plays the same role. Desire, and in particular sexual desire, appears on the scene through other means than the direct representation of the genitals and is quite the opposite of perversion in a clinical sense. Perverse sexuality, to the contrary, requires particular overvalued objects (a fetish, for example) and only those elements provide satisfaction. In normal sexuality, a fetish may inflame and excite desire. It gives an occasion for the sexual aim to begin and to end. A fetish could be a costume or a shirt or some shoes. In normal sexuality, a costume, or a shirt or a pair of shoes, forms the circumstances that bring partners to sexual satisfaction. In perverse fetishism, the normal sexual aim is replaced by the fetish in such a way that one partner overvalues the costume and fixates his or her satisfaction around that costume. The sexual object might wear the costume to inflame desire, but that desire stops at the costume and does not proceed to the normal sexual aim. Perverse fetishism is derailed sexuality that is exclusively given over to the attractive force of the costume. The shoe fetishist, for example, will prefer the shoe to the body of the partner.

The essay on the aberrations illustrates an important element of psychoanalysis and its significance for literary criticism. The normal and the pathological dimensions of human life – what we will see below described as clinical anthropology – are discussed together as possible expressions of human life and desire. In the passages I have so far discussed from *The Studies on Hysteria* or *The Interpretation of Dreams,* I have emphasised that psychoanalysis does not regard the difference between the pathological and the normal as a matter of quality but of quantity or intensity. The continuity between the sick and the well is further confirmed in the theory of sexuality where normal and perverse sexuality belong to the same set of possible paths of sex and desire. The potential for perversion is built into human sexuality as is the potential for illness or health. Freud aims to understand human life by understanding its various possible forms from the perspective of his clinical work, rather than from the perspective of an ideal of human health or, what is worse, human morality. The forms of human life that Freud describes allow us to consider how to live well in human communities. As a treatment, psychoanalysis helps those who struggle to live lives in the community, but as a theory of human life, it applies to and describes those who struggle and those who struggle less. The comprehensive approach to human life that psychoanalysis proposes suits the study of literature and culture as a particular dimension of the human struggle to make sense of daily experience and to live well in the community.

The first essay of the *Three Essays* outlines a psychoanalytic view of sexuality from the perspective of its deviances from the norm; and those deviances illustrate the norm. Freud is not the first to discuss human sexuality and sexual practice. There was an emerging discourse through the nineteenth century in Europe and elsewhere, that sought to cast a scientific eye onto all things human, including sexuality. Perhaps the most famous of these works was the Austro-German psychiatrist, Richard von Krafft-Ebing's (1840–1902) *Psychopathia Sexualis*, published in 1886. This widely influential work studied human sexual expression in clinical and forensic settings and was among the first books to treat homosexuality and bisexuality in a scientific light. While the tone of the book may appear moral and moralising, the effort to train a medical and scientific lens on human sexuality was significant and influential for Freud and others. The psychoanalytic approach to sexuality that Freud proposes also begins in the clinic, but he takes the clinical picture of sexuality to develop an approach to sexuality that is developmental across all phases of human life. This perspective proved to be controversial because it assumes that children are sexual even if their sexuality is markedly different from adult sexuality.

In the second essay, however, Freud breaks new ground by insisting that children are sexual in their thoughts and in their behaviours. In the first lines of the essay, he attacks the view that sexuality 'is absent in childhood' (SE VII 173). Sexuality is not absent in childhood, but it has been treated by writers as if it were. Freud turned to childhood sexuality because those he treated in his clinic brought it to him. In the clinic, he heard from his patients about their childhood sexual thoughts and feelings and how those thoughts and feelings came to bear on their current, adult, lives.

Freud outlines the phases of sexual expression as they circulate around the different erogenous zones of the body. He discusses the various sexual behaviours of children – thumb sucking and auto-eroticism – the pleasures that children take of their own bodies that adults try to keep them from doing. Children touch their genitals and adults try to keep them from touching them. Children engage in sometimes vigorous forms of sucking which adults encourage them to stop. In this essay, Freud outlines the notion of the erogenous zone, of the dimensions of infantile sexuality and their places in sexual development, the notion of polymorphous perversity, sublimation and others. The theory of infantile sexuality helps us understand the variety of human pleasures and can help literary critics understand the structures of desire and pleasure, of deprivation and pain that literature represents.

Erogenous zones are those sites on the body that produce pleasure and anxiety. The main erogenous zones are the eyes, the mouth, the anus and the genitals. Each erogenous zone is tied to a particular pleasure – of looking, of sucking, of expelling, and of orgasm or the sexual aim in the strict sense. Each of the main erogenous zones yields pleasure, but also risks pain and anxiety. They are not socially neutral, but invested with social and cultural importance and value. The pleasures and anxieties are not merely corporeal – they are also mental and affective. In this sense, as I have already noted, sexuality in Freud's theory is a psycho-sexuality that is tied to the body. Infantile sexuality is the basis of sexuality. The development of sexuality happens by a series of disruptions that are internal to human growth and related to education. The phases of sexuality move from oral, to anal, to genital. This means that pleasure is focused in the mouth, the anus, and then, the genitals. As we move from one phase to the next, the prior phases are not erased or overcome; instead, they are components of a total view of human sexuality and pleasure.

Polymorphous perversity is the theory that in infantile sexuality, any part of the body can become an erogenous zone. Perversity has a narrow definition in Freud's text. It refers to the sexual use of a non-sexual erogenous zone. Polymorphous perversity is not the latent expression of perversion in adult sexuality. Freud remarks that children will use any part of the body to solicit pleasure. Infantile perversity is polymorphous because it can take many forms and can shift its location from one erogenous zone to another. Polymorphous perversity illustrates the fluidity of human sexuality and desire. The thesis was scandalous when it was published as it contravened conventional conceptions of childhood in polite and public society. The contemporary belief was that children were not sexual creatures and that sexuality was a late acquisition in life. Children were not imagined to be sexual and thinking of children as sexual required a significant shift in the public imagination. It was scandalous. However, Freud built his argument from observations of children in the nursery, where expressions of sexuality are a fact of the daily life of the child. A key difference between infantile and adult sexuality is that the child does not understand its sexuality as sexual, whereas adult sexuality recognises the demands of reality and the reality principle on sexual practice. The adult has been subjected to the effects of repression, whereas the child's desire can be seen to flow freely among its varied objects.

In the oral phase, pleasure is primarily in the mouth and derived from the activity of sucking. An oral pleasure is a pleasure of seeking to become full. The infant sucks to eat and the infant's pleasure is tied first to the satisfaction of feeling full. Yet, any form of distress in the infant can trigger the desire to suck. In as much as sexuality is oral, pleasure and the regulation of anxiety is tied to the activity of the mouth and of sucking. Children will continue to suck their thumbs well into their childhood as a way to regulate their anxiety. In Freudian theory, the activity of thumb sucking – or other surrogates for the thumb, a pacifier (a fortuitous name!) – is a phase of sexual development that gives way to other phases. Oral desire does not disappear from sexuality, but takes its place as one expression among others in normal sexual behaviour and may take a prominent role in neurosis.

Freud posits two forms of infantile sexual complexes that differ in boys and girls – both of which respond to the same anxiety. The 'castration complex' and 'castration anxiety' are part of infantile sexuality that are not necessarily overcome through a process of development and maturation. Just because we get older and grow up does not mean we pass beyond castration and envy. Castration anxiety originates when children learn about the origins of life and begin to question the origins of babies. In the encounter with sexual difference, the boy begins to question the uniformity of the sexual bodies of others. Certainly, he thinks, all of us have penises. The encounter with different bodies, in particular in the nursery, leads him to an experience of anxiety about his own understanding of the world based in his bodily experience. In the famous case history of 'Little Hans', in *Analysis of a Phobia in a Five-Year Old Boy* (SE X), Freud shows how Little Hans's anxiety is articulated around Hans's understanding of the penis – what, in the case study, Hans calls a 'widdler'. The boy's castration complex revolves around his fear of losing his penis and his solution is to universalise the presence of the penis, while the castration complex for the girl centres on gaining one as the solution to anxiety.

In the anal phase of human sexual development, children attain pleasure through the withholding of stool until it can be forcibly expelled. If the oral phase is characterised by the experience of taking in, the anal is characterised by that of expulsion. Freud writes, 'Children who are making use of the susceptibility to erotogenic stimulation of the anal zone betray themselves by holding back their stool till its accumulation brings about violent muscular contractions and, as it passes through the anus, is able to produce powerful stimulation of the mucous membrane' (SE VII 186). Anal pleasure is tied to the two-fold function of withholding something and then expelling it. In the process of withholding faeces, the child begins to exercise some control over the biological process of defecation and the exercise of control differentiates the process from merely biological processes: 'One of the clearest signs of subsequent eccentricity or nervousness is to be seen when a baby obstinately refuses to empty his bowels when he is put on the pot – that is, when his nurse wants him to – and hold back that function until he himself chooses to exercise it' (SE VII 186). The anal phase is tied to the control of the body and to the regulation of pleasures in relation to others. Freud conceives of the faeces as symbolic – they are the child's first gift to the parents and later the faeces are symbolically aligned with the birth of babies (SE VII 186, 196) in the minds of children. Anal sexuality is circumscribed by secrecy, shame and filth. Anal sexuality is characterised by the act of holding on to something that is dirty and then expelling it from the body.

Anal sexuality yields developmentally to a period of latency in which nothing seems to happen with regard to infantile sexual expression until the advent of puberty. Oral and anal pleasures are pre-genital forms of sexual expression. The objects of sexual life in the oral phase of sexual development are objects that can be ingested – food, for example, or candies. In the anal organisation, differences between active and passive forms of desire appear. Anality is put into action through the act of holding on, withholding, or refusing to yield to the passivity of the anal opening (SE VII 198). The oral and anal organisations of sexuality are components of sexuality that Freud believes are brought together in the genital organisation of sexuality and oriented towards the unification of the genitals in sexual intercourse.

The picture that emerges of infantile sexuality is as a developmental process that puts different organisations or structures into play. While the genital and pre-genital (oral, anal) phases of sexuality are linked to particular developmental milestones – for example, learning to eat on one's own, potty training – they are not reducible to those moments in time. Sexuality takes these forms of organisation – oral, anal and genital. The sexual life of the adult takes these components of sexuality and draws them together as genital sexuality. The other components of sexuality are not normally eclipsed, but form part of sexual expression. Puberty inaugurates the primacy of genital sexuality, the return of genital masturbation with its attendant interdictions.

The third essay of the *Three Essays* explains the developments of genital sexuality and their relationship to infantile organisations of sexuality. The sexual phases do not pass from one to the other in the sense that they are overcome. Passing from the oral phase into the anal phase does not mean that there is no longer any oral desire. The phases of sexual development become possible lines of the expression of desire that Freud claims are unified in genital sexuality. According to Freud, genital sexuality is the finality of all sexual expression and its aim is orgasm in the service of reproduction. The psychosexuality of Freudian theory collides with a biological perspective. Later analysts and theorists note the tensions between the biological account of sexuality that seems to inhere in Freud's thought and the psychosexual theory of desire that it equally implies.

Of all of Freud's work on sexuality, the third essay problematically writes cultural-bound conceptions of gender into the theory of sexuality. So far, I have suggested that Freud's work carries with it a problematic aspiration to universality; here, those problems become most clear. Freud assumes the primacy of the penis in men and boys – a so-called, phallic sexuality – and the transformation from the external genitalia to the internal in women and girls. The male is taken to be active in his sexual expression and that activity becomes aligned with his masculinity. So the male is active and because he is active, he is 'masculine'. The same goes for women and girls: she is taken to be passive in her sexuality and because she is passive, she is 'feminine'. Freud's view begins with a sensible observation – that boys and girls experience puberty differently (SE VII 220). Boys experience puberty as an increase in libido and the over-valuation of sexual objects. All of a sudden, a boy's preferred sexual objects occupy all of his attention and everywhere he turns, he sees the object that he desires. He can only see that object as one that is worthy of admiration and devotion. The sexual object is overvalued and exulted. There are many literary examples of this process. I would point to the elevation and adoration of the beloved in any of William Shakespeare's sonnets. In those poems, the beloved is the centre and central object of the poet's imagination to the detriment of other objects. Compared to the beloved, all other things pale in value and desire. For Freud, that process describes what happens to the male in his puberty. Masculinity is, in part, due to the overvaluation of the sexual object.

Freud believes that girls do not experience the overvaluation and hyper-sexualisation of their preferred objects. In fact, the masculine dimension of overvaluation is subject to repression (SE VII 220–21). A girl becomes a woman by repressing what is masculine about her – her active relation to the objects of her sexual desire – and through repression, she becomes passive and feminine. Her sexual pleasure is relocated from the clitoris to the vagina. Men retain the value in their erogenous zones – in particular, the penis. Women's erogenous zones move from the clitoris to the vagina. 'The fact that women change their leading erogenous zone in this way, together with their wave of repression at puberty, which, as it were, puts aside their childish masculinity, are the chief determinants of the greater proneness of women to neurosis. . . .' (SE VII 221). The development of men and women seems to follow much the same course until puberty, it would seem. After puberty, women put away 'childish masculinity' whereas men come to fully express that same masculinity. Femininity therefore amounts to the repression – a defence mechanism – of masculinity in women.

Freud remarks that, 'These determinants, therefore, are intimately related to the essence of femininity' (SE VII 221). The essence of femininity, as he describes it, omits any reference to the material and social demands that women and girls experience as they age. I will only signal the objection here. Repression is a defence mechanism against psychological distress and is aimed at the maintenance of relative stability in the human mental apparatus – our thinking and our feeling. In classical psychoanalytic thought, the repression at work in this essay is understood to be an internal response to an internal anxiety. In fact, the repression may not be repression at all, but a defence against an external expectation for women and girls to conform to male expectations of femininity that are supported by the social and cultural structures in which women must live. Freud's theory of sexuality remains foundational to psychoanalytic thinking and to psychoanalytic theory and criticism. The *Three Essays* suggest the role that sexuality and desire play in human life from its origins – that all human life is sexual in its origins can hardly go unsaid and that we have often worked to hide these origins from ourselves.

The psychoanalysis of sex and gender remain a prominent site for contemporary debate in psychoanalytic theory. A student who hopes to learn more in this area could look to theorists like Joan Riviere, Melanie Klein, Nancy Chodorow, and Gayatri Chakravorty Spivak who have taken the question of women and gender as central to their literary and cultural criticism. Moreover, Jean Walton has taken up the question of race and gender in psychoanalytic theory in her book, *Fair Sex, Savage Dreams: Race, Psychoanalysis, Sexual Difference*. Walton's book links contemporary approaches to race and gender with classic psychoanalytic theory.

Culture and Society

Freud's thought was expansive in scope. He took psychoanalytic insights and applied them across a range of human experiences and to many of the problems of human communal life. In *Civilization and Its Discontents* (SE XXI 1930), Freud examines the possibility of human happiness and satisfaction. The book is a sustained reflection on the consequences of psychoanalytic insight and the role of culture or civilisation in human life. Freud asks a simple question: is the world structured to facilitate human happiness? His thesis is a cynical one. He believes that social structures render happiness nearly impossible for human beings to attain. Everywhere we are required to renounce the actions and objects that would satisfy our desires. He writes about the conflict, obvious everywhere – the social ties that bind us together, which could be bonds of tenderness and love, are often overshadowed and overpowered by hatred and aggression. Freud writes about the 'struggle' that humans engage in with their own aggressions against each other (chapter 7), and he comes to the conclusion that we are stuck in a bind that few can escape: overwhelmed by our own sense of 'helplessness and dependence on other people, and it can best be designated as fear of loss of love' (SE XXI 124). The sense of fear and helplessness that Freud finds in culture is compounded by modernity's bureaucratic structure. Even if we struggle against the social and bureaucratic structures that govern our actions, they will still tend to displace human agency into institutions that deprive us of our satisfactions. Our will to satisfaction collides with the social order and turns human life into a struggle of internal wishes against external demands. The human subject is caught between two forces and is pressured by both to renounce its pleasure and the result is illness or misery.

Freud ends his elaboration into the question of human happiness with a clear sense of the stakes of his thought in the particular historical moment at which he writes: 'The fateful question for the human species seems to me to be whether and to what extent their cultural development will succeed in mastering the disturbance of their communal life by the human instinct of aggression and self-destruction' (SE XXI 145). For all his late cynicism, Freud also affirmed the great heights that humans are capable of feeling and achieving. Though the book closes with his scepticism about our future as a species – that is, will we be able to overcome our aggressive impulses or not – the book opens with a description of the most peaceable feeling of integration in the universe.

The first chapter of *Civilization and Its Discontents* is a famous reflection based on a letter that Freud received from his friend, Romain Rolland, a French novelist, writer and intellectual who was awarded the Nobel Prize in Literature in 1915. Rolland wrote to Freud in response to Freud's book, *The Future of an Illusion*. In that book, Freud argues that monotheistic religions are illusions that are constructed on the image of the idealised father who is displaced from this world to eternal life in heaven. We hold on to this illusion as a way to cope with the reality of our lives and disappointments. Nonetheless, religion is an illusion. Rolland writes to Freud about a particular feeling that humans experience, which he calls the 'oceanic feeling'. 'It is a feeling he would like to call a sensation of "eternity," a feeling as of something limitless, unbounded – as it were, "oceanic"' (SE XXI 64). The 'oceanic feeling' is a feeling of eternity, a sense of harmony and integration of the self and the world. When one feels the 'oceanic feeling', one feels as if everything in the world aligns with the good and that he/she is part of it. Freud adds that Rolland insists that while the feeling is a 'subjective fact', that is, he reports that it is with him much of the time and that while it is not in itself a religious feeling, it is at the source of the 'religious energy' that different religions and churches 'channel' into different ends. The 'oceanic feeling' is the feeling that is sublimated into religious activity. Freud is critical of that activity even as he recognises its potential for cultural achievement. Freud's thought in *Civilization and Its Discontents* takes place between these two forces – between the destructive power of aggression and the human creative potential. In much of Freud's thought, we find the human being as a being bound between its own destructive drives and its potential for high achievement. Human life is a struggle between these and the struggle is psychological and affective, public and social.

Ego, Super-ego, Id

Psychoanalysis operates on the basic division of mental life into conscious processes and the unconscious. In *The Interpretation of Dreams*, Freud thinks of this division in a primarily 'topological' way. He conceives of the human mind in the spatial metaphor of topography in which the conscious mental system is divided from the unconscious one. This is a common division that we can now easily understand. The unconscious is further divided between the 'unconscious' and the 'preconscious'. Some elements of the unconscious pass more easily into conscious thought than do others. The preconscious consists of all of those thoughts and memories that are not actively in conscious thought but which can easily become conscious when they are triggered by a thought, a suggestion, a comment in conversation, a reminder. These are often things that we have forgotten, or wish we have forgotten, but their presence in our consciousness does not pose a significant risk to our well-being. Those thoughts and feelings that come easily to mind, even if they are uncomfortable, are preconscious. In the unconscious are those thoughts, fantasies, or wishes that, were they to be directly expressed in consciousness, would give rise to considerable distress. For example, incestuous wishes or aggressive impulses towards one's parents or brothers and sisters are often too difficult for the consciousness to bear and they remain unconscious through the mechanism of repression. We run a considerable risk of pain if we entertain aggressive thoughts and feelings towards our parents or brothers or sisters for too long or if we too openly declare these thoughts. Regardless, we harbour aggressive wishes and thoughts towards those we are supposed to love – our parents, our partners. We are able to hold on to these thoughts only if we remove them from consciousness, unless we find a way to express those same feelings without risking too much pain. If we hold on to them and do not give them any expression, their dangerous power increases and they become all the more intolerable to conscious or preconscious thought.

Even in his early work, Freud thought about human mental functioning in a dynamic way. That is, he thought about the unconscious in dynamic terms as a wishing machine. As his thought developed over time, he came to emphasise the dynamic conception of the mind and developed a second topography in 1923, in *The Ego and the Id*. It is in this book that the classic Freudian terminology becomes fully systematised in terms that are perhaps most famous in psychoanalysis: Ego, Super-Ego, Id. Freud systematises the terms in this book, but he had been using these terms in his work for some time. The Ego is what we know as the conscious ego. The Ego is the I that is conscious of itself as an I. The Id is Freud's name for the dynamic unconscious. The Super-Ego is a part of the Ego that contains the idealisations of the Ego and, for this reason, is also known as the Ego-Ideal. The Super-Ego develops in us through the experience of the family romance or the Oedipus complex. In the Oedipal situation, the child wishes to obtain all of the satisfactions attached to his preferred parent. The child wishes to be the one and only adored of that parent, to take that parent as his own or her own:

> The child's parents, and especially his father, were perceived as the obstacle to a realization of his Oedipus wishes; so his infantile ego fortified itself for the carrying out of the repression by erecting this same obstacle within itself. It borrowed the strength to do this, so to speak, from the father. (SE XIX 34)

Freud assumes the Oedipus complex (SE XIX 33) on clinical grounds and its resolution helps to account for the installation of the Super-Ego in the ego as a kind of 'categorical imperative' (SE XIX 35). The 'categorical imperative' is a term that comes from the ethical philosophy of Immanuel Kant (1724–1804). For Kant, the categorical imperative is a formulation of the moral law that will be valid in any and all circumstances without contradiction. In psychoanalytic terms,

> The super-ego retains the character of the father, while the more powerful the Oedipus complex was and the more rapidly it succumbed to repression (under the influence of authority, religious teaching, schooling and reading), the stricter will be the domination of the super-ego over the ego later on—in the form of conscience or perhaps an unconscious sense of guilt. (SE XIX 33)

The Super-Ego is installed in the mind as the force of the moral law that is acquired through the dissolution of the Oedipus complex. The conception of the mind that emerges in Freud's thought is a dynamic process of inter-relations among the Id – the primary process unconscious that wishes – the Ego where conscious thought takes place and the Super-Ego that demands the ego conform to the prescriptions of the law.

The psychoanalytic conception of the mind, and of the drama of human development, opens spaces for literary and cultural critics to situate the works that we study in the context of the human practices that the texts represent. Psychoanalytic criticism and theory that attend to the mental, cultural, historic and mythological dimensions of the literary text allow us a way to understand the inter-subjective situation of literature, which, by its very nature, puts an audience into relations with a text and with others. The psychoanalytic description of mental life allows literary critics to understand the ways in which the representations that we read and study map onto broader human experience and processes. We find our mothers or our fathers, our sisters and ourselves, and through that processes, come to find solutions to the conflicts that are part of all human communities.

Death and the Death Drive

Freud published *Beyond the Pleasure Principle* in 1920 and this slim book contains, perhaps, the most difficult Freudian thesis. In this book, Freud questions a basic and puzzling structure of neurosis. Freud observes that some neurotics seem to repeat the same behaviours over and over even when those behaviours seem to accomplish very little and that those behaviours are very difficult to stop. They seem to be less agential actions, that is, actions over which a subject has some autonomous control, and are more like compulsions. These behaviours are exemplars of a compulsion to repeat. This is the psychoanalytical concept of the repetition compulsion. Freud does not develop this theory by way of reference to his neurotic patients, but through one of his preferred sets of examples, from observations of children's play. Psychoanalysis asserts that much of adult life can be traced to childhood structures; and that as we age, we retain significant elements of our infantile concerns and habits. Consequently, to understand adults, we can start by understanding children. Moreover, Freud asserts that much of neurosis can be linked to infantile structures that have developed in a pathological way.

In *Beyond the Pleasure Principle*, Freud describes a game that he observes in the case of a child with whose parents he had been staying. The child, at the age of about eighteen months, would throw little toys into a corner of his room and then seek them out again. As he found the toys, he would give a loud 'oooh' (SE XVIII 14). Freud surmises that the game that the child is playing – the famous 'Fort/Da' – is a game of 'disappearance and return' (SE XVIII 15). What happens in the game is that a cherished object

– a toy – is disappeared so that it can be found again and with it, the child's pleasure returns. The painful event is a necessary prelude to the pleasurable one. Freud takes his interpretation further still: 'At the outset he was in a *passive* situation – he was overpowered by the experience; but by repeating it, unpleasurable though it was, he took on an *active* part' (SE XVIII 16). The game is the child's way to appropriate his agency relative to his cherished object – he takes control over his world even if just through a game and even as the game requires him to experience pain in the first instance. In this example, the child's play operates under the basic guidance of the pleasure principle which demands that the most unpleasurable experience be brought into conformity with it.

The case of the child's play is relatively straightforward – but what of those who seem to repeat behaviours like the child's but who do not gain any modicum of control over those feelings of loss and whose efforts to overcome them seem to produce more pain? In his work with patients, Freud saw this consistently and that led him to postulate that there was a force more ancient in the mind than the pleasure principle – a force that is indeed, beyond the pleasure principle, a force that manifests itself in the compulsion to repeat. Freud postulated this as a mental drive that aims to take us to a point of zero mental excitation – a death drive (SE XVIII 36). The death drive is Freud's speculative account of how the repetition compulsion takes those who suffer further and further afield from those elements and activities of life that produce pleasure and which make it possible to live with relatively less misery. Freud is pessimistic about of the possibilities of human happiness, as we have seen. In the thesis about the death drive, he suggests that there is in us an ancient force that drives us towards death, the drive to bring about an earlier state of zero mental excitation.

In literary criticism, the importance of the death drive and of the repetition compulsion appears when literary texts repeat particular signs and symbols and when those signs and symbols take on an absolute quality that suggests there is nothing beyond the sign or symbol. Death, as we know, is a constant theme in literary texts from nearly all times and all places. A psychoanalytic approach to literary texts from the perspective of the death drive is less concerned with the images of death and dying than with the horizons for action in the face of death. The death drive is death become necessity and resignation. In the grips of the repetition compulsion, the subject is in a condition of inertia where her agency disappears as agency and the character becomes a character who is, perhaps, nearly dead already and who desires nothing but death.

Wild Analysis and a Future for Psychoanalytic Criticism

In a brief essay in 1910, '"Wild" Psychoanalysis', Freud describes a case in which he received a referral to his practice from a physician, who knew of psychoanalysis but did not understand its theory or its practice. The physician's patient came to Freud with another woman, somewhat older than she, and in Freud's description, she showed her age. The woman who was referred to him was experiencing severe anxiety, was in her forties and going through a divorce. Her anxiety had become so intense that she consulted her physician who told her that her problem was related to her sexual dissatisfaction and that she must go back to her husband, take a lover, or start masturbating if she wanted to be relieved of her condition. As Freud notes, the physician knew enough of psychoanalysis to know that the anxiety and neurosis have sexual origins, but he clearly did not understand the psychoanalytic conception of sexuality. Her physician understood some of the claims, but did not understand the theory. He believed that her problem was in her sexual life (SE X 222) and if the problem is in the sexual life, the solution to the problem must also be sexual, hence his assessment: go back to your husband, take a lover, or masturbate. Since psychoanalysis says that neurosis can have a sexual origin, then a change to sexual practice can affect and ameliorate the symptoms. Freud notes that the physician is, indeed, mistaken.

Psychoanalysis does claim that human development is sexual, but the psychoanalytical theory of human sexuality is that it is a 'psychosexuality'. That means that the development of human psychology must account for the cognitive and affective side of human development. The psychosexual account of sexuality precludes the kind of direct link of sexual practice to emotional life that the lady's physician suggests to her. If emotional life and sexual behaviour were so easily linked, the clinic would require less talk and more action outside the consulting room. The fact that psychoanalysis cures through talking signifies the complexity of the link between our emotional and mental life and the symptoms we feel in our bodies. To be psychosexual means that our loves and desires and our bodies form a whole that will be well or ill depending on an entire range of factors in and beyond our control.

The woman's physician errs again in failing to see the actual onset of her illness. He sees it as the emerging absence of sexual activity and he prescribes as treatment the return to sexual practice. If the lady had experienced some actual neurosis – anxiety neurosis, neurasthenia, some traumatic event or circumstance – an actual disruption in her mental and emotional life that was directly linked to some proximate, precipitating cause, then, perhaps a somatic response would be prescribable as the proper course of treatment. Her physician does not pursue that line of inquiry and does not consider that the onset of the illness may have a psychological rather than somatic stimulus. That is, she may have a neurotic response to the psychological difficulty, a response that she feels in her body as anxiety though there is not a physical or somatic source. Her physician does not see the difference between the somatic and the psychological.

The referring physician is perhaps right to refer her to Freud, but is ill-informed in his reasoning. He sees a woman suffering from anxiety and in his acquaintance with psychoanalysis, makes a judgment and a referral to Freud. He has an insufficient theoretical understanding of psychoanalysis. The wild psychoanalyst – the treating physician who knows enough to send his patient to Freud but does not know enough of the theoretical elaboration of psychoanalysis to understand how to treat his patient – makes scientific or theoretical errors that lead to a failure of the treatment, or technical errors (SE X 225). The technical error that Freud finds is among the most common – psychoanalysis looks for and reveals the hidden motivations of our loves and desires. What we most dearly want is often hidden from us and, in and through analysis, those secret wishes and desires can be revealed to us. Those with limited theoretical knowledge may believe that the process is over with the revelation of the wishes. The analyst helps the patient to see the hidden truth of their desire and then the affliction is lifted. The physician thinks that once he has revealed the sexual nature of the affliction, and once sexual life is resumed, the affliction will be over. He believes that possessing some knowledge is enough to make the circumstances of a life better – as if knowing the nature of the problem would be sufficient to heal or to cure. The practice of psychoanalysis suggests otherwise. The analyst cannot simply inform the patient what is wrong with him or her and what is the cause of the suffering and by that revelation relieve the patient of the suffering. In fact, as his patient does, when told directly of the source of their suffering, the patient is as likely to revolt and disrupt the possibility of carrying out the analysis any further. Freud writes, 'if knowledge about the unconscious were as important for the patient as people inexperienced in psychoanalysis imagine, listening to lectures or books would be enough to cure him' (SE X 225). Lectures and books are not enough to bring about a cure. Wild psychoanalysis is that kind of analysis that proceeds from the cursory insights of psychoanalysis without the theoretical and clinical base that can anchor the speculations and interpretations that the analyst offers to the analysand. Psychoanalysis can heal, but as a wild practice, as any insufficiently theoretical undertaking, the wild analysts interventions will fail to bear the force of truth in the patient's illness and to heal. Its recommendations for treatment are outlandish, ineffective, even dangerous. At the same time, as psychoanalysis has the tendency to go wild, it is precisely that savage quality that produces inventive and theoretically grounded critical work in a variety of fields.

A Clinical Anthropology

In the contemporary world, psychoanalysis exists on a broad stage and has been appropriated in many disciplines as a theory and method for understanding human thought, feeling and behaviour. Tomas Geyskens and Philippe Van Haute reinterpret psychoanalysis as a clinical anthropology. By this, the Belgian psychoanalysts assert that psychoanalysis is not reducible either to a model of therapeutic intervention or high theoretical speculation. Psychoanalysis is not a metaphysics or an ontology that produces a truth or even truths. It cannot promise to tell us a theory of everything. Nothing in psychoanalysis is universally and eternally true. It does not ask for or promise the truth, the whole truth and nothing but the truth. For all that it might not be, psychoanalysis does promise to allow us to hear, if we would listen, the experience of desire. The anthropological perspective does not come from outside of the clinic, but from inside. Geyskens and Van Haute claim, 'Freudian psychoanalysis is indeed a *clinical* anthropology. To study the fundamental dimensions of human existence, it consults the pathological variants. . . . Pathology reveals the hidden structure of normality, which must be examined from the perspective of these fault lines' (*From Death Instinct to Attachment Theory* xi). Psychoanalysis is an anthropological endeavour of the broadest kind and is not to be mistaken for the modern discipline of anthropology. Psychoanalysis looks at the breaks and fissures of normal human life – of the lives of humans who are able to live with relative ease in the world as they experience it. Indeed, what is normal is what is most common or most shared. Most people are able to live without major disturbances that impede their ability to live and to function and when most experience a deep pain or loss, the most common experience is to find a way through. For those that struggle to find a way through the pains of existence, psychoanalysis can help in practical and theoretical ways. Practically, psychoanalysis helps in the clinical field when real, suffering people seek help. Theoretically, it can be instructive in illustrating, particularly, human ways of living, acting and surviving.

Psychoanalysis approaches what is fundamental in and to our desire and we might claim to speak truly of desire or of our own desires, but it is not in the name of psychoanalysis that we speak the truth, since in the name of psychoanalysis we are asked only to speak. Psychoanalysis takes us to the limit of experience, in the clinic and out, to trace the bedrock and the processes that make us the animals that we are now. Freud's discovery and the interventions by later analysts such as Jacques Lacan (1901–81), Jean Laplanche (1924–2012), Melanie Klein (1882–1960), Donald Woods Winnicott (1896–1971) and others offer a comprehensive anthropology informed by the experience of the clinic. For people who suffer through their days, it promises a reprieve – not happiness, but a reprieve – from the suffering that constitutes and occupies them. The picture of the healthy human originates in the stories of those whose lives have become unmanageable, unbearable, or just plain dull, and who wind up in an analyst's office, a therapist's waiting room. From those stories and those stories alone Freud was able to develop an anthropological picture of human happiness and suffering. In this view of psychoanalysis, we do not begin with a set of theoretical principles but with and through the work of the clinic. This anthropology is not an ideal or idealised formal, ontological and epistemological structure or system. The psychoanalytical anthropology that the clinic has generated remains open to further elaboration and modification. It is supple in ways that resists dogmatism even if psychoanalysis has run the risk of becoming dogmatic. This does not mean that we disregard certain concepts that psychoanalysts have developed through their clinical work. What we avoid are the dogmatisms of application that have plagued much of psychoanalytic literary, film and cultural criticism. Too often, psychoanalytically informed criticism and theory is accused, however fairly or unfairly, of a dogmatic obscurantism that favours jargon over plain speech and common ways of talking. I am sympathetic to this criticism, even if I believe that the picture it paints is itself a distortion born of an ill-considered (usually unconsidered) theoretical commitment. If we are ready to listen, psychoanalysis can teach us quite a lot about who we are. By linking psychoanalytic stories to the history of literature, we can continue to build the sense of who we are and how we relate to one another.

Chapter Two

Dreams and Psychoanalytic Theory and Criticism

A close reading of chapter 7 of *The Interpretation of Dreams* will give the student interested in psychoanalytic thought an entering wedge into such strange things as the unconscious, desire and dreams. To this end, I begin with a discussion of Freud's notion of the unconscious and of consciousness. In chapter 1, we have seen the broad strokes of Freud's work and some of its key terms and themes. In what will come now, we will see Freud's thought unfold in a more systematic and sustained way. Though it was one of Freud's first major works of psychoanalysis, *The Interpretation of Dreams* remains a foundational work for both the theory and the application of psychoanalytic thinking to human experiences. After outlining the Freudian unconscious, as it is explained in *The Interpretation of Dreams*, I will move to a discussion of dreams and to the processes that form dreams: condensation, displacement, representation and revision. I will concentrate on the fundamental terms of Freud's understanding of dreams, in particular the division of the dream into its manifest and latent contents and the dream as a fulfilment of a wish. Then, I will take a dream that Freud himself analyses and show how his insights can apply to that dream. The strategy for interpreting a dream is the same strategy that literary critics ought to adopt – and which I will adopt below – in interpreting literary texts.

The core of the psychoanalytic understanding of the mind lies in Freud's description of the unconscious. One of the major tasks of his work as a theorist and clinician was to describe the structure and operation of the unconscious. The unconscious is not reducible to the negation of consciousness. A common sense way of understanding the unconscious is inadequate to understand what Freud means by this term. To understand Freud's idea of the unconscious, we should understand the totality of human mental and psychological life – the whole of our 'mental apparatus' – as a structure of two distinguishable parts: consciousness and the unconscious. Freud observes that there are things that happen in our mental lives that consciousness cannot account for, such as dreams, slips of the tongue or pen, and other apparently innocuous mistakes.

Consciousness and the unconscious differ as we can observe every day in the conduct of our lives. We observe consciousness in as much as we see other people speaking, walking in the street, and as we type or eat. We are conscious of the things we are aware of. That there is consciousness is easy enough to point out. What is conscious is reducible to sense perception for Freud. He claims that consciousness plays a certain role, but, '*Only that of a sense-organ for the perception of psychical qualities*' (SE V 615). Freud here shows himself as a thinker concerned mainly with human mental life as it arises out of the deeper levels of the mental apparatus. The unconscious, however, is much more difficult to justify as a concept. As the unconscious does not appear to us as a content of consciousness, it does 'appear' directly in perception. Paradoxically, the unconscious appears without appearing, as mistakes, dreams. In this way, Freud claims that there are two distinct regions of the mind. This division is known as the 'topographical distinction' between the conscious and the unconscious. There is one mind with two different regions. Freud writes, 'The unconscious is the larger sphere, which includes within it the smaller sphere of the conscious' (SE V 612). The spatial metaphor is helpful to see how Freud understands the human psyche; he pictures it as a totality composed of the unconscious and consciousness wherein consciousness makes up a 'smaller sphere' of the unconscious.

Consciousness and the unconscious are topographically distinct, but knowing this does not help us to describe their difference in purpose and function. To understand this, we have to move to what Freud calls the 'dynamic view' of the unconscious which he revises later in his career and which I discussed above. With the topographical picture of the Freudian unconscious we can move to a discussion of what Freud means in his distinction of two psi-systems and by a primary and secondary process and the *dynamic* conception of the unconscious. Freud must distinguish the unconscious in its dynamic aspect because a topographical representation of the concept does not capture the expanse of unconscious mental functioning, and consequently, it would not be adequate to understand the dream processes.

Freud distinguishes between two mental systems. He calls them 'psi-systems' in the sense that they are psychic or mental systems. The first psi-system corresponds to the unconscious (or the *Unconscious*). The unconscious is, 'totally incapable of bringing anything disagreeable into the context of its thoughts. It is unable to do anything but wish' (SE V 600). For Freud, a wish is a mental or psychological impulse to 're-establish the situation of the original satisfaction' (SE V 565), that was present at an earlier stage of development but has since been eradicated. Freud's argument follows a developmental path on this point. Early in our lives, our mental activity is limited to 'keeping itself free from stimuli' (SE V 565). The editors of the *Standard Edition* call this 'principle of constancy'. The principle of constancy is the mental principle that the mind aims to regulate itself as having neither too much, nor too little stimulus. Freud claims that the early mental structure is like a 'reflex apparatus', and stimuli are quelled by motor action: 'sensory excitation impinging on it [the psychical apparatus] could be promptly discharged along a motor path' (SE V 565). In our early development, the mind aims to have neither too much nor too little mental stimulus. When there was an excess of stimulus, that stimulus was expressed as a bodily action. In our early development, psychical life is limited to the elimination of impulses that disrupt the principle of constancy through the body in motor operations. This level of development, however, is insufficient for dealing with the 'exigencies of life' (SE V 565), as Freud calls them, that are first confronted as 'the major somatic needs' (SE V 565). Excitations, or disruptions to the principle of constancy, are to be eliminated through movement, 'which may be described as an "internal change" or "expression of emotion"' (SE V 565). As an example Freud offers, 'A hungry baby screams or kicks helplessly' (SE V 565). The example shows how a disruption of the principle of constancy, the hunger or the discomfort of the baby, seeks resolution through movement; the baby expresses its emotion and the excitation is eliminated and the principle of constancy re-established albeit 'through outside help' (SE V 565). This change, says Freud,

> can only come about if in some way or other . . . an "experience of satisfaction" can be achieved which puts an end to the internal stimulus. An essential component of this experience of satisfaction is a particular perception (that of nourishment, in our example) the mnemic image of which remains associated thenceforward with the memory trace of the excitation produced by the need [the stimulus that disrupts the principle of constancy]. As a result of the link that has thus been established, next time this need arises a psychical impulse will at once emerge which will seek to re-cathect the mnemic image of the perception and to re-evoke the perception itself, that is to say to re-establish the situation of the original satisfaction. (SE V 565)

The 'original satisfaction' is a memory of a need that was fulfilled, of a disruption of the principle of constancy that was eventually resolved. Along with this original satisfaction goes a particular perception, the fulfilment of the need or resolution of the disruption, which is permanently associated in memory with the memory of the stimulus of the need. The hungry baby is satisfied by the mother who feeds it, instilling a kind of satisfaction in the baby. The baby's satisfaction is associated from then on with the image of its mother and the image of the mother is associated with the hunger. The next time the baby is hungry the image of the mother appears and relieves the hunger. The 'psychical impulse' that emerges when there has been a subsequent stimulus or disruption is a wish. When the child finds itself hungry again it will re-cathect or re-invest the image of the mother, which is associated with the alleviation of the stimulus and thereby tries to re-establish the situation of the original satisfaction. The wish is thus an impulse to overcome a new stimulus, but is also linked by association of memories to an original satisfaction. The wish is fulfilled with the 're-appearance of the perception' of the original satisfaction.

The first psi-system, the *Unconscious*, does nothing but wish to attain its original satisfaction. The contents of this system are memories from our earliest childhood. These memories do not lose their strength over time but they reside in this first system in a permanent way. The first system, which can only wish, is 'directed towards securing the *free discharge of the quantities of excitation*' (SE V 599, emphasis added). This means that the first system seeks to get what it wants and what it wants is to maintain itself in a state of equilibrium; it wants to maintain the principle of constancy. It wants to take excitations or stimuli and do away with them because the gathering of excitations, is, according to Freud, a source of 'unpleasure'. Thus, in a state of unpleasure that results from an accumulation of stimulation, this system seeks to eliminate the unpleasure by engaging in an activity that alleviates the unpleasure. This is sought through wishing, through a desire to bring about the state of the original satisfaction. In the case of dreams, the first system gets its satisfaction in the hallucinatory image as 'the memory of satisfaction' (SE V 600); the original satisfaction is attained through the hallucination.

The mental apparatus is divided into two systems, as we have discussed: the unconscious and the preconscious. What is unconscious is fully inadmissible to consciousness, whereas what is preconscious may enter into consciousness. While the unconscious is totally barred from entering into consciousness, the preconscious on the contrary, mediates between the unconscious and consciousness. 'We have described the relations of the two systems to each other and to consciousness by saying that the system *Preconscious* stands like a screen between the system *Unconscious* and consciousness' (SE V 615), says Freud. The excitations of the preconscious can move into consciousness, after observing certain rules; rules that make the contents of the preconscious acceptable to consciousness.

While the first system can only wish and is satisfied by the hallucinatory dream image, it cannot be so quelled forever. Satisfaction through hallucination is not sustainable to the point that would permanently satisfy the wishes of the first system. The second psi-system corresponding to the *Preconscious* works against the memory material in the first system. Where the first system seeks a 'free discharge', the second system invests that energy in such a way that it manages to 'inhibit' the discharge (SE V 601); the preconscious is a censoring power. The second system, 'cathects [invests] memories in such a way that there is an inhibition of their discharge, including, therefore, an inhibition of discharge . . . in the direction of the development of unpleasure' (SE V 601). The second system blocks the wishes of the first system that seeks their fulfilment. The unconscious, however, never tires of wishing and will find a way to make the wishes acceptable to consciousness so that there is a silencing of the stimulus, a fulfilment of the wish that is acceptable to the censoring activity of the preconscious. This second system is a censoring system and is for Freud, the 'key to the whole theory of repression' (SE V 604). In this way, one can see the mental apparatus, as Freud conceives it, as two separate powers: the unconscious which seeks the re-establishment of an original satisfaction and the preconscious that limits the wishing power of the unconscious.

We can distinguish two separate processes that are appropriate to each system. A 'primary process' is a psychical process that is possible in the first system and a 'secondary process' is the sort of process that 'results from the inhibition imposed by the second system' (SE V 601). A primary process is 'primary' in two senses: importance and chronology. That is, the primary process (a process the apparatus of which Freud calls a 'theoretical fiction' for no apparatus exists that exhibits only a primary process) is chronologically prior to the secondary processes. Freud says, 'the primary processes are present in the mental apparatus from the first, while it is only during the course of life that the secondary processes unfold, and come to inhibit and overlay the primary ones' (SE V 603). The unconscious functions according to primary processes; it seeks its satisfaction continually and is only inhibited by the development of the censoring secondary processes. Hence, to sum up, we have according to Freud, two psi-systems, the unconscious that can only wish, and it functions only according to the rules of a primary process. The preconscious is the agent of repression. Consciousness is only a sense organ and it perceives the qualities of psychical life.

With these observations, we have another picture of the unconscious as a dynamic force in psychical life. The unconscious, as a dynamic force, functions according to an economics of psychical excitation and investment to that is opposed to the preconscious system that censors the wishes of the unconscious and the primary processes according to the demands of reality. Freud uses the study of dreams to establish this understanding of psychical life. I have decided to proceed in an opposite way to facilitate my presentation of Freud's analysis of dreams.

Perhaps one of the most beautiful aspects of Freud's book is its synthetic aim. Freud claims to account for the totality of thinking about dreams in the West, and in that tradition, he rejects only two accounts of dreams. He rejects the idea that dreams are meaningless and that dreaming itself is a meaningless or nonsensical mental event. Contrary to that view, Freud believes that dreams lead us to the core of human thinking. The second thesis about dreams that Freud rejects is that they are reducible to a somatic process. Indeed, for Freud, a dream is a psychical event of no less importance than any other psychical event. In fact, 'the interpretation of dreams is the royal road to a knowledge of the unconscious activities of the mind' (SE V 608), the knowledge which is Freud's central aim. By studying dreams, we learn about the unconscious. By understanding the unconscious, we understand ourselves.

A dream is a form of thought in which ideas are transformed into hallucinations; a dream 'dramatises' an idea. The dream has two contents. There is what the dream appears to be, its manifest content, and there is the underlying dream thought, its latent content. According to Freud the novelty of his approach is that all previous attempts to understand the phenomenon of dreaming has attempted to do so based on the 'manifest content as it is presented in our memory' (SE V 381). This ignores the distinction between the manifest content of the dream and the latent dream thoughts.

Consequently, the interpretation of a dream will be, 'the task . . . of investigating the relations between the manifest content of dreams and the latent dream-thoughts . . . and of tracing out the processes by which the latter have been changed into the former' (SE V 381). The task is thus two-fold. On the one hand, the analyst will have to find the relations between manifest content, what the dreamer dreams, and the unconscious thoughts that underlie the dream. On the other hand, the processes by which the dream thoughts are transformed into the manifest content of the dream must also be articulated. According to Freud, the most important of these processes are 'condensation' and 'displacement'. Under the title of 'The Dream-Work', Freud undertakes an analysis of these processes.

Briefly, condensation is that process by which different and varying elements of the dream thoughts are brought together into one element. Displacement is the work that takes the dream thoughts that have a 'high psychical value and strips them of their intensity and on the other hand, *by means of over determination*, creates from elements of low psychical value new values, which afterwards find their way into the dream-content' (SE V 417, emphasis added). Displacement erases thoughts that have a high value and moves the intensity of the value to things that have little or no value. Condensation and displacement are the two central means by which latent thoughts are transformed into the manifest content of the dream. The form that dreams take may be attributed essentially to these processes.

A dream is always a fulfilment of a wish. This is clear for Freud even in the earlier chapters of the book: 'When the work of interpretation has been completed, we perceive that a dream is the fulfilment of a wish' (SE IV 121). This presents a few problems for Freud's theory of dreams, problems that he fully acknowledges – for example, anxiety dreams. But passing over that difficulty (which Freud has an answer for), Freud sees that there is a division in the way the wish is fulfilled in the dream. Either the wish is openly fulfilled or the wish that is fulfilled is totally unrecognisable in the dream. In the first case, Freud points to the dreams of children which are often 'pure wish-fulfillments and are in that case quite uninteresting compared with the dreams of adults' (SE IV 127). But he also points to a very simple dream that we all have from time to time. Freud writes,

> I dream I am swallowing down water in great gulps, and it has the delicious taste that nothing can equal but a cool drink when one is parched with thirst. Then I wake up and have to have a real drink. This simple dream is occasioned by the thirst which I become aware of when I wake. The thirst gives rise to a wish to drink, and the dream shows me that wish fulfilled. In doing so it is performing a function. . . . (SE IV 123)

The function that this simple dream performs is to maintain sleep and fulfil the wish to drink.

In another sort of dream, wish fulfilments are hidden from direct view. In such dreams, the latent dream thought is distorted or censored. Freud writes, 'in cases where the wish-fulfilment is unrecognizable, where it has been disguised, there must have existed some inclination to put up a defence against the wish' (SE IV 141). This inclination is the censorship and it works by transforming the dream thoughts either in the work of condensation or especially in the work of displacement. My next step will be to explicate Freud's account of the origins of wishes that 'come true in dreams' (SE V 551).

Freud distinguishes between three origins of wishes in dreams:

1. The wish may have been aroused during the day and for external reasons may not have been satisfied; in that case, an acknowledged wish which has not been dealt with is left over for the night.
2. The wish may have arisen during the day but been repudiated; in that case, what is left over is a wish which has not been dealt with but has been suppressed.
3. The wish may have no connection with daytime life and be one of those wishes which only emerge from the suppressed part of the mind and become active in us at night. (quotation modified, SE V 551)

Now, dreams arise from the unconscious and so it is necessary to recall the picture of the mental apparatus that I have sketched out above. Freud locates the wishes that belong to the first of the three origins in the preconscious since thoughts in the preconscious can easily move into consciousness. Such wishes consequently belong to the functional domain of the secondary process of repression; although the repression is not fully actualised and the wish can pass into and out of consciousness with no problems whatsoever. The wishes of the second origin have been pushed from the preconscious to the unconscious where they reside permanently and can come into consciousness only if they can be invested in such a way so that the unconscious wish can attach itself to an image that is acceptable to the censorship of the preconscious. The wishes of the third origin belong to the unconscious and are 'altogether incapable of passing beyond it' (SE V 551). To this list Freud adds a fourth possible origin, namely, those wishes that come about in the course of the night, like thirst, for example.

So far I have dealt mainly with the formal aspects of the formation of dreams. I have touched on the work of condensation and displacement, that dreams are fulfilments of wishes and all of this against the backdrop of Freud's main discovery and aim, the explication of the unconscious. Next, I will introduce the effective instigators of dreams.

That dreams are fulfilments of wishes is clear. A dream, however, must have an effective cause. A conscious wish is not necessarily forceful enough to cause a dream on its own according to Freud and the preconscious wish must find some 'reinforcement from elsewhere' (SE V 553). This 'elsewhere' is the unconscious; Freud's 'supposition is that a conscious wish can only become a dream-instigator if it succeeds in awakening an unconscious wish with the same tenor and in obtaining reinforcement from it' (SE V 553). The *Preconscious* functions as a screen between the *Unconscious*, which is a timeless store of memory that wishes in a continual way, and consciousness which is a mere sense organ for psychical qualities. Thus, a wish that is conscious may 'contribute' (SE V 553) to the dream, but is not forceful enough to cause the dream. If the conscious wish is to appear in a dream, it will have to find some support from the unconscious so that the unconscious wish, which may belong to the preconscious or the unconscious, and the conscious wish coincide. For Freud, unconscious wishes are always present and always looking for a means of discharge and fulfilment. They are 'ready at any time to find their way to expression when an opportunity arises for allying themselves with an impulse from the conscious and for transferring their own great intensity on to the latter's lesser one' (SE V 553). Unconscious and conscious wishes are of differing strengths and the weaker conscious wishes give an opportunity for the intense unconscious wish to express itself in the dream and consequently it will '*appear* as though the conscious wish alone had been realised in the dream' (SE V 553, emphasis added). Freud emphasises the 'appear' because to end the analysis of the dream with what appears is to limit the analysis to only one part of the dream: the manifest content. As I have shown above, this is only one aspect of the dream and not the aspect that Freud is mainly interested in; the latent content, the dream-thoughts, is what the interpretation of dreams aims to uncover and thereby understand the unconscious wish at work in the dream.

At this point we have read enough of Freud's theory to attempt an interpretation of a dream. The dream I will take up is the famous 'dream of Irma's injection' and following Freud's lead, I will reproduce it in full here and then discuss Freud's interpretation of it.

> *A large hall—numerous guests, whom we were receiving. —Among them was Irma. I at once took her on one side, as though to answer her letter and to reproach her for not having accepted my 'solution' yet. I said to her: 'If you still get pains, it's really only your fault.' She replied: 'If you only knew what pains I've got now in my throat and stomach and abdomen—it's choking me.' —I was alarmed and looked at her. She looked pale and puffy. I thought to myself that after all I must be missing some organic trouble. I took her to the window and looked down her throat, and she showed signs of recalcitrance, like women with artificial dentures. I thought to myself that there was really no need for her to do that. —She then opened her mouth properly and on the right I found a big white patch; at another place I saw extensive whitish gray scabs upon some remarkable curly structures which were evidently modeled on the turbinal bones of the nose. —I at once called in Dr. M., and he repeated the examination and confirmed it. . . . Dr. M. looked*

> *quite different from usual; he was very pale, he walked with a limp and his chin was clean-shaven. . . . My friend Otto was now standing beside her as well, and my friend Leopold was perusing her through her bodice and saying: 'She has a dull area low down on the left.' He also indicated that a portion of the skin on the left shoulder was infiltrated. (I noticed this, just as he did, in spite of her dress.) . . . M. said: 'There's no doubt it's an infection, but no matter; dysentery will supervene and the toxin will be eliminated.' . . . We were directly aware, too, of the origin of the infection. Not long before, when she was feeling unwell, my friend Otto had given her an injection of a preparation of propyl, propyls . . . propionic acid . . . trimethylamin (and I saw before me the formula for this printed in heavy type). . . . Injections of that sort ought not to be made so thoughtlessly. . . . And probably the syringe had not been clean.* (SE IV 107)

Now, although the dream is reported as a continuous narrative, the analysis of the dream cannot be undertaken as if it were. In order to gain access to the underlying wishes in the dream, we have to penetrate beneath the manifest content of the dream and discover the latent dream thoughts. To do this, each image of the dream has to be analysed and put into the context of the dreamers recent history, in this case, Freud's recent history. But this would not be enough; we need also the dreamer's associations to the dream images. These associations are the thoughts that occur to the dreamer over the course of reflection or reporting of the dream, and as will be seen, are often linguistic, which at least suggests a link between the unconscious and language.

Freud explains the first image of the dream, the large hall with many guests, as originating from the large house where he and his family would be spending their summer. Freud anticipated his wife's birthday in this dream, 'on the previous day [she] had told [him] that she expected a number of friends' (SE IV108). Among those friends would be Irma, Freud's patient. We can see immediately how the dream-work takes hold of recent conscious experience, the day's residues, and uses them as the media through which the dream thoughts will be represented. It is important for this dream that Freud says Irma will be present because as we will see, Freud's unconscious wishing circles around his relationship with Irma.

Next, in his dream, Freud reproaches Irma for not having accepted his solution to her symptoms. He says to her, 'If you still get pains, it's your own fault' (SE IV 108). The speech in the dream is important because it is Freud's view that speeches in dreams are derived from words actually spoken in waking life (SE IV 271). That Freud may have actually said this to his patient is quite possible, he says, for at that time, he was of the opinion that all his duty as a psychoanalyst was to inform the patient of the 'hidden meaning' (SE IV 108) of her or his symptoms and the cure was obtained. Freud did not 'consider himself responsible' for whether or not the patient 'accepted the solution', although 'this was what success depended on' (SE IV 108). But Freud attaches more meaning to these words he spoke to Irma in his dream. He says that he held the unconscious wish to be absolved from the responsibility for the pains she still had. That the psychoanalytic therapy did not cure Irma was not because Freud was inept, but because Irma would not accept what the therapy had to offer. With this we see the first inclinations of the purpose and meaning of this dream. Freud the dreamer does not want to be responsible for Irma's continued illness despite the apparent failure of the psychoanalytic treatment and thus we pierce for the first time beneath the manifest content of the dream. In his interpretation, Freud expresses this possible interpretation as a question, 'Could it be that the purpose of the dream lay in this direction?' (SE IV 109).

The next part of the dream to be interpreted are Irma's pains as Freud represented them in his dream. He says that stomach pains were not among the most important part of Irma's symptoms and that 'choking' pains in her throat 'played scarcely any part in her illness' (SE IV 109). Freud cannot come up with any reason why he represented Irma's pains in this way; one could say that it is not important to come up with any precise explanation of the origins of these representations – that there is some pain is all that matters. This can be seen as an example of displacement. His patient's pain would carry too much meaning, have too much value and so they are moved from their location in real life, to another more innocuous place. Further, that Irma looked strange in the dream does not seem to be so important for Freud at this point in the interpretation; he gives only one sentence to it saying that he suspected that someone else was being substituted for Irma in the dream. This is the first hint of a possible condensation and an indication that more than one person is being represented as 'Irma' in the dream. Because of the work of displacement and condensation, one image in a dream can be filled with significations that in waking life can never be made. An excellent example is that of Freud's dream where he sees his uncle with a yellow beard. In this dream, Freud dreams of his friend R. but dreams of him as his own uncle with a yellow beard, his Uncle Josef, the simpleton. In the case of the dream of Irma, Freud does not go further along these lines.

The next part of the dream that Freud gives an explanation for is his alarm that Irma's illness may indeed be organic. For a psychoanalyst this worry is warranted, especially, says Freud, 'to a specialist whose practice is almost limited to neurotic patients and who is in the habit of attributing to hysteria a great number of symptoms which other physicians treat as organic' (SE IV 109). But there is another side as well; in his dream, Freud has his doubts. If her symptoms were organic, that is all the better for him because Freud is only a psychoanalyst and cannot be held responsible for organic pain. The analyst's primary concern is the conversion of psychical pain into bodily symptoms or hysterical pains. At this point in the interpretation, Freud states directly what he sees as one of the dream wishes behind the manifest content of the dream, 'I was actually *wishing*,' says Freud, 'that there had been a wrong diagnosis; for, if so, the blame for my lack of success would also have been got rid of' (SE IV 109). This is the first time that Freud states what he finds as one of the unconscious wishes that underlies this dream, although it has already been hinted at. It is important to note that there is nothing in the manifest content of the dream that should suggest this meaning; rather, it is only in the process of analysis that the underlying dream thoughts are brought to light. The wish that Freud finds here is acted out in the dream; that is, the unconscious finds some satisfaction in the wish being expressed in a dream, although in waking life it would be impossible to maintain. Because dreaming is what Freud calls a primary process, it is not subject to the kind of censorship that our waking life, which is subject to the secondary process of repression, is subject to. Consequently, in the dream, all sorts of wishes can be tolerated and expressed that in waking life we would find repulsive, impossible, or even unthinkable.

In the next portion of the dream, Freud sees himself examining Irma's mouth. This is strange for Freud because never had he looked into Irma's mouth. What he finds here is a memory of carrying out the same examination on a governess who appeared young and beautiful but had false teeth. This is another example of condensation; the two women are combined into one and the same representation. This detail does not take on a great importance for the analysis of the dream but is another good illustration of how the dream-work does not obey the rules of waking life; many memories can be condensed by the dream-work into one dream image in the manifest content of the dream. Freud says that there was no need for the 'recalcitrance' that Irma displayed in her resistance to his effort to look at her mouth, which he considers as a compliment to Irma, but thinks that there is a further meaning as well. Freud recalls that he had seen another woman, the patient of a Dr M, whom he expected was also a hysteric but who was also 'an intimate woman friend' (SE IV 110) of Irma. This woman's symptoms, which were diagnosed by Dr M as a diptheritic membrane, were choking, the same symptom exhibited by Irma in Freud's dream. Thus the condensation of Irma, the governess, and now, Irma's friend is evident, and the symptoms that were represented in this dream are not only the product of a displacement, but also of the condensation exercised by the dream process. This brings us to a second wish hiding in Freud's dream; namely, Freud had 'played' (SE IV 110) with the idea that this woman would come to him for help. Thus, a desire which had been conscious, but subsequently forgotten, was revived in the dream thoughts, which is one of the possible effective origins of a dream, as discussed above.

Another woman finds her way into Freud's interpretation of this dream. The 'bad' teeth remind him of another woman whom he did not want as a patient because he thought that she would not be 'amenable' (SE IV 110) to treatment. 'She was usually pale, and once, while she had been in specially good health, she had looked puffy' (SE IV 110. In the dream thoughts, then, Freud says, he was comparing Irma to the patient of Dr M and the other woman (who is associated with Freud's wife in a footnote), both 'people who would also have been recalcitrant to treatment' (SE IV 110). This leads Freud to find a third wish in his dream. He would have liked to exchange Irma for her friend. 'For Irma seemed to [him] foolish because she had not accepted [his] solution' (SE IV 110). Irma's friend would have made a much better patient because she would be more amenable to the treatment, or so goes Freud's wish. 'She would then have opened her mouth properly, and have told [him] more than Irma' (SE IV 110).

Freud's analysis has so far revealed three wishes, all more or less similar. He finds that he is not responsible for Irma's continued illness, that he wishes he could swap Irma for her friend, and he finds that Irma remains responsible for her illness because she did not properly 'open her mouth' the way her friend would have. These wishes that underlie the manifest dream are accessible only through the process of interpretation and are, according to *The Interpretation of Dreams*, the only way to make dreams intelligible. Indeed, that is the purpose of his book – to show that the way in which dreams have heretofore been regarded does not explain the phenomenon in an adequate way, and to offer a way of understanding dreams that is novel and yet still accounts for the insights that the long tradition of dream interpretation has come up with.

The next portion of the dream explained takes the interpretation further away from Irma. The white patch in Irma's throat 'reminds him of diphtheritis and so of Irma's friend, but also of a serious illness of my eldest daughter's' (SE IV 111). This brings him to the worries that he had of his own health due to cocaine use and also the illness developed by a woman patient of his who had developed a nasal infection due to extensive use of cocaine. Further, the misuse of the drug had killed a friend of his, an episode that will return later in the dream. These associations remain merely associations in the context of Freud's analysis; he does not pursue them to arrive at the dream thoughts that underlie the images of the manifest dream. What we do see here is how the dream content is derived from the recent history of the dreamer.

The next portion of the dream – where Freud called in Dr M who repeated the examination of Irma's mouth – recalls for Freud a time when he had to call in a senior physician to look at a patient who had taken a turn for the worse under Freud's care. This patient, who eventually died, is significant for Freud, because she had the same name as his oldest daughter, Mathilde. This shows how associations can work along linguistic lines; two persons are associatively linked in someone's mind because they share a name. Freud attributes this to a process of unconscious self-accusation; he was accusing himself of being unconscientious as a medical practitioner: 'it seemed as if I had been collecting all the occasions which I could bring up against myself as evidence of lack of medical conscientiousness' (SE IV 112). The image of Dr M as he appeared in the dream is another condensation of two people: Dr M who indeed appeared pale and Freud's brother who was clean-shaven and walked with a limp. The unconscious fused the two together in the dream via condensation because both had rejected suggestions he had made to each of them and for this Freud harboured some resentment towards them. The dream gave an opportunity for this resentment to be expressed. This goes together with an earlier wish Freud uncovered in this dream, although Freud does not go into this in his interpretation of the dream: namely, the wish to be listened to and his advice accepted. He had avenged himself on Irma, her continued illness was not his fault, and now was reasserting that his advice is valuable to two others who had recently rejected it.

The next portion of the dream compares two of Freud's friends, Otto and Leopold. They are both physicians in the same field but have differing characters. Otto is quick and clever while Leopold is slower, deliberate and prudent. Freud sees his dream as comparing Irma, the disobedient patient, to her friend who would be more amenable to his treatment; and on the other side, as making a similar comparison between Otto and Leopold, 'to the advantage of the latter' (SE IV 112). Freud does not further elaborate on this comparison; he simply says that it is present in his dream. Now, what the doctors all see is that there is an 'infiltration' on Irma's shoulder, a detail that Freud relates to the pain he has in his own shoulder. This is an example of the displacement in the dream:

his own pain is given to someone else. As the examination of Irma continues, a distinction is observed in the manner of examining children and of examining adult, women patients. Children can be examined without their clothes on, while women have to be examined through their clothing. This is how Freud explains the portion of the dream, 'in spite of her dress'. However, he cuts the analysis off abruptly, saying, 'Further than this I could not see. Frankly, I had no desire to penetrate more deeply at this point' (SE IV 113). Arguments trying to explain Freud's hesitance at this point could be given, but are not the point of this chapter.

'Dr. M. said: "It's an infection, but no matter. Dysentery will supervene and the toxin will be eliminated"' (SE IV 113). The reference to the infection is a reference to Freud's daughter's illness and the fact that Leopold had informed him of the presence of an infection like the one that appeared in the dream. But the infection, although it pained Irma, was of little consequence. Freud's dream again tries to move the blame from himself and attribute its cause to an organic process: if she suffered an organic disease, then Freud would be exonerated. The fact that his treatment failed would be of little matter because 'psychological treatment could not be held responsible for the persistence of diphtheritic pains' (SE IV 113). In the dream, Freud receives reassurance from Dr M that Irma's problem is not grave, that in the end it will be eliminated. The manner of the elimination appears ridiculous to Freud, but he associates it with another patient that he had not taken on, 'a young man with remarkable difficulties associated with defecating' (SE IV 115). The association is linguistic and turns on the word 'dysentery'. Another association that Freud gives involves Dr M. Several years earlier, Dr M had been called in for a consultation on a seriously ill patient whose own doctor had taken a 'very optimistic view' regarding his health. Freud says that this portion of the dream, it cannot be doubted, expresses his 'derision of physicians who are ignorant of hysteria' (SE IV 116). Further, Freud sees the dream as accusing Dr M of being duped by the hysteria of Irma's friend. But, Freud asks, why does the dream treat his friend, Dr M, so poorly? Because Dr M disagreed with his solution to Irma's illness as much as Irma herself disagreed with it. Thus, the dream seeks revenge on two people in Freud's life: on Irma and Dr M, and it does this by attributing Irma's continued illness to her own refusal of the solution and by putting the ridiculous words into the mouth of Dr M.

All of the sudden, they all became aware of the origin of the infection and that Otto had given her an injection when she was not feeling well. This portion of the dream is not surprising for Freud, who knew that Otto had given injections to several people who were not feeling well while he was staying with Irma's family. This also recalls the friend of Freud who had killed himself with cocaine injections. Irma's injection was 'a preparation of propyl . . . propyls . . . propionic acid . . . trimethylamin' (SE IV 116), and Freud saw the formula for the trimethylamin in bold type in his dream. Freud's train of associations in this case gives the best example of how associations work in the process of interpreting the dream. The trimethylamin is important, for Freud is able to associate this substance with his friend from Berlin, Wilhelm Fliess. Trimethylamin was thought by Fliess to be important in sexual metabolism and this led Freud to think of sexuality. The association goes from 'trimethylamin', to 'Fliess', to Fliess's thesis, to 'sexuality'. Sexuality is then associated with Irma, who is a young widow. And, 'if I wanted to find an excuse for the failure of my treatment in her case, what could I best appeal to would no doubt be this fact of her widowhood' (SE IV 116–17). The trimethylamin is important because it leads Freud to consider sexuality in general, Irma's sexuality in particular, and further it reveals how the dream sought out an ally who agreed with Freud against Irma and Dr M in his attempt at the cure.

'Injections of that sort ought not to be made so thoughtlessly.' Coming to the end of the analysis, Freud says that he was further blaming Otto for the ease with which he reaches conclusions without giving them proper consideration. Freud also finds here a reference to his friend who died of cocaine injections. What does Freud gain in accusing Otto? Two things: he finds evidence for his conscientiousness and affirms that he is a good doctor, that he would never give an injection of this sort without ample forethought. Second, he finds evidence of his unconscientiousness, 'touching upon the story of the unfortunate Mathilde' (SE IV 117), whom he had poisoned with repeated injections of sulphonal. And there is another accusation that Freud's dream levels against Otto, 'and probably the syringe had not been clean.' Freud reports that in two years he had not caused an infection because of a dirty syringe and he was proud of this; he is conscientious. He discovers this by a report to him that an old woman whom he gave injections twice a week had come down with phlebitis that Freud immediately attributed to a dirty syringe. The presence of phlebitis leads him to think of his wife, who had an illness during one of her pregnancies. Then, three unreported memories he had of his wife, Irma, and his dead patient, Mathilde, 'enabled [him] to substitute the three figures for one another in the dream' (SE IV 117). He does not say what these memories are, only that their association made it possible in the course of the dream to substitute one person for another.

Freud's analysis of his dream ends here. The somewhat belaboured and highly repetitive exposition that I have tried to give here was not intended to deepen Freud's original interpretation or to criticise it in places where it was lacking or where Freud backed off from taking his interpretation to its fullest ends. Rather, my intent was to highlight the functioning of the critical tools that Freud discussed in the later part of his book and especially in the final chapter. Overall, my aim with this chapter is to provide an entering wedge into psychoanalytic thought. The benefits of this exercise are many, but to give only one example, Freudian suspicion, the searching for causes beneath the apparent, forces a reader into careful scrutiny of texts. That is, not on a clinical but a theoretical level, a reader who has appropriated a psychoanalytical perspective to a text can try to interpret the text in much the same way as Freud interpreted his dream, which he reproduced as a text. There are serious limits to such a perspective. With a text, we have no access to the author's associations, nor to her or his recent history in detail. The dimensions of the clinical methods of psychoanalysis are not available to literary criticism and theory. The text is not a person who can sit with the analyst and speak.

Nonetheless, the associations of the terms used in a literary text, like the terms of the dream text, are a fruitful place for an interpreter of a text. They allow the theoretical knowledge that psychoanalysts have developed from Freud's work, and sometimes in opposition to it, to be used as a useful hermeneutical option to interpret a text. An understanding of Freud's texts is foundational to such an interpretation.

Chapter Three

Psychoanalysis and Literature

Literary references abound in the development of psychoanalytic writing. As I have noted, and is clear from many of Freud's texts, psychoanalysis and literature are bound together because so many of psychoanalysis' examples are literary ones. Literary examples suit psychoanalysis because so much of literature circulates around the problems that humans encounter over the course of their lives. Literature is, among other things, the imaginary representation of human problems and human struggles. It is also an effort to find ways to live through or to solve those same problems. Problems with mothers and fathers, fights with brothers and sisters, friends and lovers, husbands and wives are the stuff of literature. Literature deals with the conflicts of human life and the solutions that humans seek to mitigate those conflicts. The conflicts are not just external – a fight between a father and a child, for example, or the struggle of a mother and a daughter and the rivalries and joys of living in a family. The conflicts are also hidden within us – how we secretly think and feel about those conflicts. Psychoanalysts since Freud have looked to the history of literature as a place for examples and models of human living. The primary literary narrative that psychoanalysis addresses is the Ancient Greek story of Oedipus by Sophocles.

Freud often wrote about literature and he was a voracious reader of literature. In addition to the clinical and theoretical works that I described in chapter 1, he wrote many works in which he engaged with literary texts to advance the theoretical and clinical claims of psychoanalysis. In 1919, he published an essay, 'The Uncanny', that described the experience of 'the return of the repressed' by analysing a short story by the German author E. T. A. Hoffman (1776–1822), 'The Sandman'. You may know Hoffman as the writer of the famous Tchaikovski ballet, 'The Nutcracker'. Hoffman's tales were full of gothic images and atmosphere that were very popular in nineteenth century Europe. In his essay, Freud engages with the notion of the uncanny, a category of aesthetic feelings associated with what is scary and frightening and which is familiar to people across cultures. In German, the word for uncanny is '*unheimlich'*. The 'un' of the word is the same as in English. The 'lich' is equivalent to the English 'ly'. 'Heim' indicates 'home'. In this way, we can understand Freud's '*unheimlich*' as 'un-home-ly'. Freud elaborates on his argument about the uncanny from this linguistic perspective. He will use the word to show that those things that are uncanny are most familiar to us like those things that are close to home. In this sense, uncanny would mean, unfamiliar (SE XVII 221).

Freud constructs his argument about the uncanny through a detailed reading of the lexicography of the word in several European languages and he settles on a definition that comes from the German philosopher Friedrich Wilhelm Joseph Schelling (1775–1854): 'According to him, everything is [uncanny] that ought to have remained hidden but has come to light' (SE XVIII 225). The feeling of the uncanny will turn on the experience of a revelation of something that ought not be seen or be known. The experience of the uncanny is the experience of a shudder or of a fright at seeing something one is not supposed to see. Hoffman's tale is about 'The Sandman' who is used as a threat – 'On certain evenings his mother used to send the children to bed early, warning them that "the Sand-Man was coming"' (SE XVII 227). The Sand-Man was a threat uttered by the mother to change the children's behaviour – to get them to bed. The mother means the threat innocently, but the nurse elaborates on the fantasy:

> He's a wicked man who comes when children won't go to bed, and throws handfuls of sand in their eyes so that they jump

> out of their heads all bleeding. Then he puts the eyes in a sack and carries them off to the half-moon to feed his children. They sit up there in their nest, and their beaks are hooked like owls' beaks, and they use them to peck up naughty boys' and girls' eyes with. (SE XVII 228).

The Sand-Man is a fantasy figure who disciplines children by feeding their eyes to other children who are not children, but beasts.

Freud compares the literary example to psychoanalytic experience. Children, he claims, express significant fear about their eyes and, 'Many adults retain their apprehensiveness' (SE XVII 231). Humans seem to fear damage to their eyes in a way that is more acute than the fears around other parts of the body. The eye is a site of clear vulnerability and we need only think, however briefly, of a finger or a needle touching our eyes to provoke a shudder in ourselves. Freud claims that, 'A study of dreams, phantasies, and myths has taught us that anxiety about one's eyes, the fear of going blind, is often enough a substitute for the fear of being castrated' (SE XVII 231). He turns then to the story of Oedipus, which we will see below, as one of the central stories of psychoanalysis, as an example of blindness as a sign of castration. What is uncanny in the story is the progressive elaboration of the return of castration anxiety. Castration is the infantile fear of losing one's genitals, of losing the objects that is most precious. Castration anxiety returns with the threat of losing our most precious and cherished object even if the loss is a loss in fantasy.

The uncanny is the feeling of what ought to remain hidden coming to light and it comes as a return rather than a single instance. The sense of the uncanny comes with things that return (SE XVII 241). Like the Sand-Man who makes his rounds seeking the eyes of children to feed to his own, the uncanny is marked by a feeling of fright that returns when we come to see what we ought not to have seen. What is uncanny is not new; it is 'familiar and old-established in the mind and which has become alienated from it only through the process of repression' (SE XVII 241). The figure of the Sand-Man is the return of the castration anxiety. Castration anxiety is the dread of losing something that we wish not to lose and which, in reality, we never have lost, though the anxiety around the threat of loss never yields. It returns as something that should remain hidden but has come into light. The uncanny is a literary feeling that we find wherever we find darkness and dread, wherever we find what we should not find. It is a feeling of slight shudder – a familiar feeling of things being not quite right. It is a feeling that nags and returns when least we expect it, like in the night when we hope to go to sleep.

While psychoanalytic critics can, and have, written about nearly every literary text imaginable, Freud continues to return to the same ones: the texts about Oedipus and Hamlet. Even the discussion in 'The Uncanny' returns to Oedipus. Shoshana Felman calls Oedipus the 'specimen story of psychoanalysis' (99). The story of Oedipus is a mythical story of intergenerational conflict driven by jealousy, love and ambition. When Sophocles wrote the tragedy, which was first performed in Athens in 429 BCE, the story was already ancient. It is a 'family story'. It was predicted that the King of Thebes, Laius, would be dethroned and murdered by his son. In an effort to outrun his fate, when a son is born to his wife, Jocasta, Laius gives the infant to a servant. The infant's feet are clubbed so that he will hobble rather than walk, and he is taken to a mountain to be left to die, exposed on the hillside. The servant cannot leave the infant to die, as is understandable. After all, the infant is an infant, and overtaken by compassion, is given over to a shepherd to be raised as his own. Laius and Jocasta go along their lives, believing themselves saved from their fate. If everyone plays their part as expected, Laius will not be killed by his son, whom he believes is dead, nor will Jocasta take her son as her husband. The security of their kingdom, they believe, is sound.

But, Oedipus is not dead; he grows up and he learns of his origin and his fate. What must it be like, to be a royal child and living as a shepherd. What anger he must have! What resentment must fuel his searches! He leaves the countryside and, walking on the road to Thebes, he is run off the road at a crossing by a man in a chariot. Oedipus lashes out and kills the man. He comes into Thebes, the city of his birth, that is suffering under a curse of the Sphinx. Whoever can solve the Sphinx's riddle can lift the curse and end the plague on the city. The riddle is this: what walks on four legs in the morning, on two at mid-day, and three in the evening? Answering this question will relieve the people of Thebes of their suffering. Oedipus answers the question: a man walks on four legs in the morning, he crawls as an infant; on two legs at mid-day, he walks until his old age, when he picks up a cane to support his weight.

Solving the Sphynx's riddle endears Oedipus to the people of Thebes who find in him the return of a leader who was long missing, the beloved King Laius. Oedipus marries the Queen, not knowing she is his mother nor that the man he killed on the crossroads was his father, the king. In spite of their machinations, their fates come to pass as they were prescribed – Oedipus kills his father and takes up the bed of his mother – though he does not recognise them as either father or mother. Sophocles's tragedy is built around Oedipus's basic blindness. He does not see what he does though he does it nonetheless.

Oedipus becomes the model story in the psychoanalytic account of human development because it is a story of intergenerational conflict. The son lives between two parents as rival of the father and pursuer of the mother. The son wishes he could keep his mother all to himself if only his father were out of picture. In his clinical work, Freud saw the repercussions of infantile wishes and ambivalences. On the one hand, the child loves his father. On the other hand, if the father were absent, gone, or dead, the child could have the mother all to himself. The aggressive wish and the tender and loving feeling towards the father can coexist but for a short time. The aggression will be subjected to repression as a defence mechanism. It is too difficult for the tender affections of a son to abide with the urge to have the mother all to himself. The Oedipus complex takes place in and among the network of wishes and repressions of aggressive impulses towards the child's deepest love objects – his mother and his father.

Freud discusses the Oedipus story at length in *The Interpretation of Dreams* and there he treats the story in the context of his discussion on the sources of dreams. He suggests that the wishes that Sophocles's tragedy puts on stage are wishes that modern spectators, like ancient ones, share (SE IV 262). Freud summarises the situation like this:

> It is the fate of us all, perhaps, to direct our first sexual impulse towards our mother and our first murderous wish against our father. Our dreams convince us that this is so. King Oedipus, who slew his father Laius and married his mother Jocasta, merely shows us the fulfillment of our own childhood wishes. But, more fortunate than he, we have meanwhile succeeded in so far as we have not become psychoneurotics, in detaching our sexual impulses from our mothers and forgetting our jealousy of our fathers. Here is one in whom these primaeval wishes of our childhood have been fulfilled, and we shrink back from him with the whole force of the repression by which those wishes have since that time been held down within us. While the poet, as he unravels the past brings to light the guilt of Oedipus, he is at the same time compelling us to recognize our own inner minds, in which those same impulses, though suppressed, are still to be found. (SE IV 262–63)

This long passage illustrates many of the fundamental elements of the Oedipus complex. First, the Oedipus complex has the feel of necessity or fate. The life of the human subject has a kind of inner determination. That inner determination is the primary process of the unconscious and it is formed by the world into which the child is born. In our dream life, Freud asserts and demonstrates, our hidden wishes can be ascertained and studied. In the family story, the roles of mother, father and child are crucial and Freud's account of them, in this passage, emphasises the story from the perspective of the child. The child – a boy – loves his mother and is jealous of his father and out of that jealousy, the 'first murderous' wishes emerge. The jealousy for the father is expressed as aggression and a wish to have the mother all to himself.

In normal development, however, the child is able to disentangle his early, infantile love for his mother and his aggressive impulses towards his father in developing relationships with others and finding a place for himself in the world. Though coming from and through a family structure that is similar to the mythic story of Oedipus, the child overcomes those early determinations. The child seems fated to repeat the structures of his family, but he manages to disentangle his own life from his family's. The child has to detach himself from the family. In 'Family Romances', Freud calls this process a difficult and necessary one. 'The liberation of an individual, as he grows up, from the authority of his parents is one of the most necessary though one of the most painful results brought about by the course of his development' (SE IX 237). The Oedipus complex is the ground from which the human subject emerges and it appears to be one dominated and determined by fate or necessity. If we are to be free, though, we have to detach from that ground and break out of the fate we appear to inherit from our families.

The family story of Oedipus dominates much of psychoanalytic theory and criticism. As the specimen story of psychoanalysis, it becomes a model for analytic interpretation.

Freud's insights into literary texts were later adapted and developed by other thinkers and critics. Shoshana Felman develops an approach to psychoanalytic criticism that emphasises psychoanalysis as a way of reading – she develops this account of reading in and through her own reading of Freud. She is part of a generation of literary critics who were among the first to be influenced by structuralism and by the work of Jacques Lacan. The structuralist critics – influenced by the emergence of the structural linguistics of Ferdinand de Saussure in Switzerland and of Russian Formalism – looked to literary texts as structures that could be interpreted in their component parts. Structuralists looked to the linguistic elements of texts that could be isolated and compared with other texts. Jacques Lacan (1901–81) was a French psychoanalyst who was also influenced by structuralist criticism in his readings of Freud. He conducted a seminar on Freud's texts from 1953 until 1980. His interpretation of Freud – what he called a return to Freud – influenced an entire generation of literary critics and theorists around the world. Felman's own critical voice emerges from the confluence of structuralism (that tends towards poststructuralism) and Lacanian psychoanalysis.

Felman approaches criticism as a theory of reading. The development of her version of psychoanalytic criticism follows Freud and Lacan as readers – Freud as a reader of literature and of the unconscious (Felman 23–24) and Lacan as a reader of Freud. She puts these readings into practice in a reading of Edgar Allan Poe's texts. The choice for Poe is over-determined. Indeed, Lacan decides to frame the only book he wrote – his *Ecrits* (1966) – with his seminar presentation on Poe's story, 'The Purloined Letter'. Freud engaged literature from the very beginning in developing psychoanalysis, as I have emphasised throughout. Lacan frames part of his return to Freud in and through a reading of Poe's story. Felman argues that Lacan's revision of Freud amounts to an insistence that Freud's discovery is a 'practical discovery of a new way of reading' (23). Felman's contribution to psychoanalytic criticism is to show how psychoanalytic critics have read literary texts. She discusses the criticism on Poe's works as a way to engage with psychoanalytic readings of literary texts and then to illustrate the difference that she believes that psychoanalytic reading makes in the writing of literary criticism.

Felman discusses three ways of reading psychoanalytically by following the moves of three psychoanalytic approaches to Poe's texts and she uses the psychoanalytic genre of the case study as her model. She reads a critical work on Poe by Joseph Wood Krutch whose *Edgar Allan Poe: A Study in Genius* (1926) treats Poe's text as 'nothing other than an accurate transcription of a severe neurosis' (Felman 32) and which she describes as an 'evaluative approach' to literature. She then moves to a book by Marie Bonaparte, *The Life and Works of Edgar Allan Poe: A Psychoanalytic Interpretation* (1934, trans. 1937), as a model of reading psychoanalytically that treats the author as an extension of the works; what she calls a 'clinical diagnostic' approach to literature (35). Finally, she comes to Lacan whom she sees as the preferred model of psychoanalytic reading that she calls 'textual problematization' (39).

In his work on Poe, Joseph Wood Krutch (1893–1970) reads the literary text as a way to understand the author. Krutch asserts that since Poe's works are not like people's lives, the only approach that makes sense is to look to Poe's biography as a way to explain how the grotesque and macabre texts come into being. Poe's stories are so gruesome – many of them – that they can only be the fruit of a sick imagination (Felman 32–33).

> Krutch thus diagnoses in Poe a pathological condition of sexual impotence, the result of a fixation on his mother, and explains Poe's literary drive as a desire to compensate for, on the one

> hand, the loss of social position of which his foster father had deprived him and, on the other hand, his incapacity to have normal sexual relations, through the creation of a fictional world of horror and destruction where he found refuge. (33)

Krutch's method is the first issue. He moves from the content of the narratives to an explanation of how they must have come to be. What he does not do is subject those narrative elements to the methods of psychoanalysis in which the objects that appear in a narrative are the reworked images of wishes. That is, Krutch reads Poe's texts as if he were reading the fully disclosed latent dream thoughts and not the manifest content of the dream – if we take dream interpretation as a model of psychoanalytic interpretation. Krutch is left with an interpretation of Poe that is 'reductionist, stereotypical simplification' (33) that 'renders this approach inadequate' (33) to the demands, rigours and complexity of Poe's art. To evaluate the psychology of the artist through their art is a reductive use of psychoanalytic methods that amounts to a short-sighted use of Freudian insights and methods. This is a kind of criticism that is like the 'wild psychoanalysis' I discussed above. Like the referring physician in Freud's text, Krutch understands enough of psychoanalytic theory to miss the mark in his writing about Poe and his art. Nonetheless, it is a style of psychoanalytic reading and criticism that sometimes still appears in print and often appears in works that aim to caricature or denigrate psychoanalytic thought. As Felman notes, if psychoanalysis can be used to turn Poe into a psychotic rather than an artist, then, 'Krutch . . . reduces not just Poe but analysis itself into an ideologically biased and psychologically opinionated caricature, missing totally . . . the radicality of Freud's psychoanalytic insights (35). One of the risks of psychoanalytic criticism is reductionism or wild psychoanalytic criticism.

Marie Bonaparte (1882–1962) was an early follower of Freud and one of the first women psychoanalysts. Her work on Poe is instructive in its application of psychoanalytic concepts to literary texts as a way to diagnose what is pathological in Poe in order to understand the pathological mind. Whereas the approach of normative evaluation sets out to judge, the approach of clinical diagnosis sets out to understand and to explicate pathology.

Bonaparte goes about her reading of Poe with care and attention to Poe's texts and to psychoanalytic concepts and insight. She uses the poetry and the stories as a way to enter Poe's unconscious. The approach is a type of applied psychoanalysis that might be supple and nuanced in its application of psychoanalysis, but tends to be rigid and reductive to the literary text. In applied psychoanalysis, the text becomes a mere example of knowledge that the critic already has. Felman argues that, 'In setting out to expose didactically the methods of psychoanalytic interpretation, Bonaparte's pioneering book at the same time exemplifies the very naivete of competence, the distinctive professional crudity of what has come to be the classical psychoanalytic treatment of literary texts' (36). Indeed, for those who have some training in psychoanalytic theory, Bonaparte's book has the feel, today, of being entirely predictable. We seem to know what the interpretations will be. This is not to denigrate its accomplishment at the moment of its publication when these interpretations were not quite as expected; it does, however, indicate the extent to which systematic interpretations fixed psychoanalytic knowledge as a given set of interpretations at the very same time that Freud described the unconscious as a dynamic – rather than fixed – dimension of the mind. It is difficult to reconcile the dynamism of the unconscious with the rigidity of Bonaparte's interpretations.

If Krutch's evaluative approach is reductive both to psychoanalysis and literature, Bonaparte's classical diagnostic approach is reductive to literature and risks the 'crudity' of dogmatism. Two risks, then, of psychoanalytic criticism have been reductionism and dogmatism. Felman proposes Lacan's style of reading as a way of reading psychoanalytically that avoids both reductionism and dogmatism. Felman calls Lacan's style of psychoanalytic reading 'textual problematization' (39). Lacan's texts are understood to be dense, baroque, frequently obscure and notoriously difficult. In following Felman's teaching of Lacan's style of psychoanalytic reading, I hope to suggest a practical way of reading psychoanalytically. Felman lists five differences between Lacan's reading of Poe and Bonaparte's classical interpretation. Rather than focus on Lacan's theoretical apparatus, through which he reads Freud and Poe, I will focus on the practical moves that Felman has found in Lacan's 'Seminar on the Purloined Letter'.

'The Purloined Letter' is a short story by Poe in the detective genre. In Poe's imaginative universe, C. Auguste Dupin is a famous detective in Paris and has been engaged by the prefect of the police to find a letter that has been stolen from the Queen's bureau. The letter is not from the king, but from her paramour. The prefect has done everything he knows to do to find the letter, but to no avail. The task that the prefect presents is to find the letter without disclosing to the king the contents of the letter or alarming the one who stole the letter into disclosing its contents. The queen is being blackmailed and the prefect of the police is charged with ending it. This is the problem: to return the letter to the queen without allowing the one who stole the letter to know that it has been returned. We should see already the psychoanalytic emphasis on objects that return and on behaviours that are repetitions. Felman lists the five differences between classical psychoanalytic reading and Lacanian reading as matters of interpretation of the repetition compulsion (44), as an emphasis on the signifier rather than the signified (44–46), a textual rather than a biographical approach (46), a subversion of the relation between author and analyst (46–49), and implication of psychoanalysis rather than its application (49).

The 'repetition compulsion' is a central concept in psychoanalysis. In *Beyond the Pleasure Principle,* Freud describes the compulsion to repeat or the 'repetition compulsion' as a dimension of human behaviour and thought that cannot be explained by the regulation of the 'pleasure principle'. According to the pleasure principle, the human subject aims to maintain an ideal of excitation – neither too much nor too little. In conflict with the 'reality principle', the human subject seeks ways to satisfy its drives without causing too much pain or risking too much distress. The pleasure principle aims to keep the human in a relatively stable situation. In neurosis, Freud observes a cycle of repetition in which the neurotic repeats a behaviour or thought. The repetitive behaviour can become so intense that it intrudes into the neurotics' life and becomes the source of their suffering. The repeated behaviour or thought is symptomatic and is not a pleasurable experience.

Freud describes some of these behaviours of his patients: 'None of these things can have produced pleasure in the past. . . . They are of course the activities of instincts intended to lead to satisfaction; but no lesson has been learnt from the old experience of these activities having led instead only to unpleasure. In spite of that they are repeated, under pressure of a compulsion' (SE XVIII 21). Freud speculates that there is a more primitive, more primary compulsion to repeat that 'overrides' the pleasure principle, which he believed, in *The Interpretation of Dreams*, to regulate thinking and wishing.

Lacan's theory of reading begins with the notion of the repetition compulsion. Whereas Freud's observations of the compulsion to repeat imply a repetition of the same – the same word, act, gesture or behaviour – Felman shows that for Lacan, the repetition compulsion appears as a difference. 'The Purloined Letter' is a story of displacements where the letter remains the same, but its place in the narrative shifts. Every time the letter appears, it appears as a difference rather than an identity. First, it is on the Queen's bureau, then it is on the bulletin board, and then it is in Dupin's hands. When it appears, it takes a different value relative to its place. Repetition is not repetition of the same or of identity, but the compulsion to differentiation. As Felman suggests, 'the significance of the letter is situated in its displacement, that is, in its repetitive movements to a different place' (44). The value of the letter changes each time it changes hands. Classic psychoanalysis interprets the repetition compulsion as the repetition of the same and it fails to observe the way in which language inscribes the symptom but cannot contain it. That is, naming the symptom does not fix it, but displaces it like the letter moving among its addressees.

The second Lacanian difference in reading bears on the notion of the signifier. Lacan was influenced by the structural linguistics of Ferdinand de Saussure whose account of language divided the linguistic sign into the signifier and the signified. The signified is the cognitive content of the sign. The signifier is the materiality of the sign. The signifier has no necessary cognitive content. In the strictest sense, it has no meaning except in as much as it would refer to another signifier but instead of having a signified to anchor its meaning to some non-material content, it acquires its value by differentiation from other signifiers. When Felman claims that Lacanian reading is marked by an insistence on the signifier as opposed to an analysis of the signified, she insists on Lacan's psychoanalytic reading of Poe as 'itself an allegory of the psychoanalytic reading' (44). Felman compares Lacan's approach to Bonaparte's. Bonaparte aims to understand the letter as a content of the unconscious that can be linked to Poe's biography. In Poe's story, the police search for the letter in every conceivable place in the apartment where they know it to be. They insert needles into the sofas; they look in the legs of the chairs for hollows where the letter might be rolled up and inserted. The police believe that they will find it if they just look hard enough. Felman links the methods of the police to Bonaparte's method. She believes that she can disclose the real thing of the letter. Bonaparte looks for the signified.

Lacan's approach is to emphasise the signifier. Felman rightly believes that reading for the signifier can be found described in *The Interpretation of Dreams* where the dream images are read without any necessary connection to the cognitive content of the terms that the dreamer uses in reporting the dream. In the analysis of a dream, the dream images are not important in their own right, but in how they point to other images and the associations that the dreamer puts on those images. This emphasis, Felman says, is 'a radical reversal of the traditional expectations involved in the common psychoanalytical approach to literature and its invariable search for hidden meanings' (45). In Lacanian reading, the meanings are not hidden and the meanings are not even the only object of reading. Reading the signifier instead of the signified means that we read the continuities and the disruptions in meaning. We read not only the readable – the letter as signified – as much as the unreadable – the letter as signifier. In Lacanian reading, we focus less on what the letter means and more on how the letter moves. Lacanian reading does not aim for the hidden meanings of the text, but for the signifier on the surface of the text – what the text says at the level of the signifier.

Focusing the reading on the signifier instead of the signified changes the way that we approach literature. For the Lacanian reader, the biography of the author recedes into the background and the literary text is foregrounded. Lacan offers to literary criticism a textual approach to reading instead of a biographical one. Lacan reads literary texts as a series of signifiers without predetermined cognitive content. Lacan reads what is written rather than what he presumed an author to have meant, in much the same way that Freud taught all of us to interpret dreams. On their own, dreams have very little meaning. They derive their meaning in and through the associations that the dreamer brings to the dreams. That is, the interpretation of a dream is created in the process of linking it to other dream images in the way that signifiers relate to other signifiers. Lacan approaches psychoanalysis in this way and literary critics who work in his tradition aim to approach literary texts in this way. Lacanian reading suspends judgment on the meaning of the text and instead listens for what the text says through the displacements or condensations of the signifier.

Lacanian reading undoes the priority of the author and critic. In conventional literary criticism, the critic serves the author by explicating the significance of the author's text and the critical text functions on the primary text as a kind of meta-language. The language of interpretation stands over and against the primary language of the literary text. Interpretation is mutually inflected in the text; the encounter with Poe's text changes the interpretation and the interpretation changes Poe. If we compare the Lacanian approach to criticism with other modernist criticism, we can see the difference that Lacan makes. In his seminal essay on criticism, 'Tradition and the Individual Talent' (1919), T. S. Eliot suggests that the great literary works, in their greatness, transcend their historical origins and locations. The great works of literature exist in an ideal order where classic texts interact with other classic texts and the talented poet or writer uses his historical sense to produce what is great in literature. Criticism does not affect this process and can only describe it. The poets are primary and privileged and criticism has little to do with poetry.

A Lacanian approach to literature interacts with the text and this is why it cannot be an application of psychoanalysis to literature. 'The methodological stake', Felman argues, 'is no longer that of the application of psychoanalysis to literature but, rather, of their interimplication in each other' (49). Psychoanalysis and literature have always been 'interimplicated'. However, psychoanalysis and psychoanalytic criticism were prone to reductionism and dogmatism that blocked the interrelations of literature and psychoanalysis that were integral to Freud's work. Many analysts approached literature with psychoanalysis as a way of explaining literature, in much the same way that Eliot tried to explain the great talents of poetry. They assumed that the literary text would remain constant and unaffected by the psychoanalytic and critical text. Yet, as a clinical practice, psychoanalysis is intersubjective and it is difficult to imagine how an intersubjective clinical discipline could be applied to another discipline without sustaining its intersubjective structure. From a methodological point of view, the failure of psychoanalytic critics, such as Krutch or Bonaparte, to sustain the intersubjective character of psychoanalysis in their criticism, shows the advantage of the Lacanian approach to literature. The interimplication of the literary text with the critical text repeats, differently, the intersubjective relation between the analyst and the analysand. Literature becomes a site of mutual interaction between text and reader, and that interaction can be the occasion of the development of new readings and new possibilities for literature. This view of literature situates literary texts in a history of engagements with writers and readers in a community of readers. Literary history is then a history of human interaction instead of a construction of an ideal order of classic artefacts.

Chapter Four

Psychoanalytic Criticism in Practice

EDGAR ALLAN POE'S 'THE CASK OF AMONTILLADO'

Before it is anything else, psychoanalytic literary and cultural criticism – criticism of film, television, media and other objects of cultural production – is criticism. That is, an effort to understand and elucidate, to question and to ponder, the claims that different kinds of texts make about the world and the people that they address. Psychoanalytic critics use the tools and methods of criticism even as they bring their theoretical commitments to bear on those tools and methods. If a critic decides to take up a psychoanalytic point of view or to immerse his or her studies of literary and cultural objects in a psychoanalytic vocabulary, he or she does not abdicate the vocabulary of literary and cultural criticism. In what follows, you will see, first, the text of Edgar Allan Poe's short story, 'The Cask of Amontillado'. After that, you will follow me as I sketch the beginnings of a possible line of psychoanalytic interpretation of the story. Psychoanalytic criticism is not a simple application of psychoanalytic ideas to literary texts. Psychoanalytic criticism ought to aim at a synthesis of psychoanalytic insight and theory and the methods of literary and cultural criticism and address at least two audiences – literary critics and readers of literary texts and psychoanalysts and psychoanalytic readers. Psychoanalytic criticism is an interaction of text and criticism in which both are changed and challenged.

Poe's story was published in 1846. The story is similar to other Poe stories in its style and atmosphere. There are gothic elements and a fascination with the macabre and with death. The story takes place in an unnamed city in Italy during a carnival. During a carnival, the normal rules that regulate social interaction are suspended. The work of daily life yields to the joy and pleasures of the celebration. Poe's theory of the short story, in which he values the effect that a story or poem produces in the reader, is on show in this story as well. It is a short, short story. Poe believed that a story ought to be brief enough to be enjoyed in an hour and it ought to produce a certain effect. In this case, I would argue, the effect is one of terror and the imagined ecstasy of revenge. Like the carnival, the story is a space where Poe's narrator and reader can play with feelings that are dangerous and outside the time of the carnival. In Poe's account of reading and writing, there is a compact between the reader and the narrator or writer. It is an intersubjective interaction. That is, the represented subjectivity of the narrator and the subjectivity of the reader, any time a text is read, operate together to produce an effect. One of the goals of psychoanalytic reading and criticism will be to describe these effects.

THE CASK OF AMONTILLADO

The thousand injuries of Fortunato I had borne as I best could, but when he ventured upon insult, I vowed revenge. You, who so well know the nature of my soul, will not suppose, however, that I gave utterance to a threat. AT LENGTH I would be avenged; this was a point definitively settled – but the very definitiveness with which it was resolved precluded the idea of risk. I must not only punish, but punish with impunity. A wrong is unredressed when retribution overtakes its redresser. It is equally unredressed when the avenger fails to make himself felt as such to him who has done the wrong.

It must be understood that neither by word nor deed had I given Fortunato cause to doubt my good will. I continued as was my wont, to smile in his face, and he did not perceive that my smile NOW was at the thought of his immolation.

He had a weak point – this Fortunato – although in other regards he was a man to be respected and even feared. He prided himself on his connoisseurship in wine. Few Italians have the true virtuoso spirit. For the most part their enthusiasm is adopted to suit the time and opportunity to practise imposture upon the British and Austrian MILLIONAIRES. In painting and gemmary, Fortunato, like his countrymen, was a quack, but in the matter of old wines he was sincere. In this respect I did not differ from him materially; I was skilful in the Italian vintages myself, and bought largely whenever I could.

It was about dusk, one evening during the supreme madness of the carnival season, that I encountered my friend. He accosted me with excessive warmth, for he had been drinking much. The man wore motley. He had on a tight-fitting parti-striped dress and his head was surmounted by the conical cap and bells. I was so pleased to see him that I thought I should never have done wringing his hand.

I said to him – "My dear Fortunato, you are luckily met. How remarkably well you are looking to-day! But I have received a pipe of what passes for Amontillado, and I have my doubts."

"How?" said he, "Amontillado? A pipe? Impossible ? And in the middle of the carnival?"

"I have my doubts," I replied; "and I was silly enough to pay the full Amontillado price without consulting you in the matter. You were not to be found, and I was fearful of losing a bargain."

"Amontillado!"

"I have my doubts."

"Amontillado!"

"And I must satisfy them."

"Amontillado!"

"As you are engaged, I am on my way to Luchesi. If anyone has a critical turn, it is he. He will tell me" –

"Luchesi cannot tell Amontillado from Sherry."

"And yet some fools will have it that his taste is a match for your own."

"Come let us go."

"Whither?"

"To your vaults."

"My friend, no; I will not impose upon your good nature. I perceive you have an engagement. Luchesi" –

"I have no engagement; come."

"My friend, no. It is not the engagement, but the severe cold with which I perceive you are afflicted . The vaults are insufferably damp. They are encrusted with nitre."

"Let us go, nevertheless. The cold is merely nothing. Amontillado! You have been imposed upon; and as for Luchesi, he cannot distinguish Sherry from Amontillado."

Thus speaking, Fortunato possessed himself of my arm. Putting on a mask of black silk and drawing a roquelaire closely about my person, I suffered him to hurry me to my palazzo.

There were no attendants at home; they had absconded to make merry in honour of the time. I had told them that I should not return until the morning and had given them explicit orders not to stir from the house. These orders were sufficient, I well knew, to insure their immediate disappearance, one and all, as soon as my back was turned.

I took from their sconces two flambeaux, and giving one to Fortunato bowed him through several suites of rooms to the archway that led into the vaults. I passed down a long and winding staircase, requesting him to be cautious as he followed. We came at length to the foot of the descent, and stood together on the damp ground of the catacombs of the Montresors.

The gait of my friend was unsteady, and the bells upon his cap jingled as he strode.

"The pipe," said he.

"It is farther on," said I; "but observe the white webwork which gleams from these cavern walls."

He turned towards me and looked into my eyes with two filmy orbs that distilled the rheum of intoxication.

"Nitre?" he asked, at length.

"Nitre," I replied. "How long have you had that cough!"

"Ugh! ugh! ugh! – ugh! ugh! ugh! – ugh! ugh! ugh! – ugh! ugh! ugh! – ugh! ugh! ugh!

My poor friend found it impossible to reply for many minutes.

"It is nothing," he said, at last.

"Come," I said, with decision, "we will go back; your health is precious. You are rich, respected, admired, beloved; you are happy as once I was. You are a man to be missed. For me it is no matter. We will go back; you will be ill and I cannot be responsible. Besides, there is Luchesi" –

"Enough," he said; "the cough is a mere nothing; it will not kill me. I shall not die of a cough."

"True – true," I replied; "and, indeed, I had no intention of alarming you unnecessarily – but you should use all proper caution. A draught of this Medoc will defend us from the damps."

Here I knocked off the neck of a bottle which I drew from a long row of its fellows that lay upon the mould.

"Drink," I said, presenting him the wine.

He raised it to his lips with a leer. He paused and nodded to me familiarly, while his bells jingled.

"I drink," he said, "to the buried that repose around us."

"And I to your long life."

He again took my arm and we proceeded.

"These vaults," he said, "are extensive."

"The Montresors," I replied, "were a great numerous family."

"I forget your arms."

"A huge human foot d'or, in a field azure; the foot crushes a serpent rampant whose fangs are imbedded in the heel."

"And the motto?"

"*Nemo me impune lacessit*."

"Good!" he said.

The wine sparkled in his eyes and the bells jingled. My own fancy grew warm with the Medoc. We had passed through walls of piled bones, with casks and puncheons intermingling, into the inmost recesses of the catacombs. I paused again, and this time I made bold to seize Fortunato by an arm above the elbow.

"The nitre!" I said: "see it increases. It hangs like moss upon the vaults. We are below the river's bed. The drops of moisture trickle among the bones. Come, we will go back ere it is too late. Your cough" –

"It is nothing" he said; "let us go on. But first, another draught of the Medoc."

I broke and reached him a flagon of De Grave. He emptied it at a breath. His eyes flashed with a fierce light. He laughed and threw the bottle upwards with a gesticulation I did not understand.

I looked at him in surprise. He repeated the movement – a grotesque one.

"You do not comprehend?" he said.

"Not I," I replied.

"Then you are not of the brotherhood."

"How?"

"You are not of the masons."

"Yes, yes," I said "yes! yes."

"You? Impossible! A mason?"

"A mason," I replied.

"A sign," he said.

"It is this," I answered, producing a trowel from beneath the folds of my roquelaire.

"You jest," he exclaimed, recoiling a few paces. "But let us proceed to the Amontillado."

"Be it so," I said, replacing the tool beneath the cloak, and again offering him my arm. He leaned upon it heavily. We continued our route in search of the Amontillado. We passed through a range of low arches, descended, passed on, and descending again, arrived at a deep crypt, in which the foulness of the air caused our flambeaux rather to glow than flame.

At the most remote end of the crypt there appeared another less spacious. Its walls had been lined with human remains piled to the vault overhead, in the fashion of the great catacombs of Paris. Three sides of this interior crypt were still ornamented in this manner. From the fourth the bones had been thrown down, and lay promiscuously upon the earth, forming at one point a mound of some size. Within the wall thus exposed by the displacing of the bones, we perceived a still interior recess, in depth about four feet, in width three, in height six or seven. It seemed to have been constructed for no especial use in itself, but formed merely the interval between two of the colossal supports of the roof of the catacombs, and was backed by one of their circumscribing walls of solid granite.

It was in vain that Fortunato, uplifting his dull torch, endeavoured to pry into the depths of the recess. Its termination the feeble light did not enable us to see.

"Proceed," I said; "herein is the Amontillado. As for Luchesi" –

"He is an ignoramus," interrupted my friend, as he stepped unsteadily forward, while I followed immediately at his heels. In an instant he had reached the extremity of the niche, and finding his progress arrested by the rock, stood stupidly bewildered . A moment more and I had fettered him to the granite. In its surface were two iron staples, distant from each other about two feet, horizontally. From one of these depended a short chain, from the other a padlock. Throwing the links about his waist, it was but the work of a few seconds to secure it. He was too much astounded to resist. Withdrawing the key I stepped back from the recess.

"Pass your hand," I said, "over the wall; you cannot help feeling the nitre. Indeed it is VERY damp. Once more let me IMPLORE you to return. No? Then I must positively leave you. But I must first render you all the little attentions in my power."

"The Amontillado!" ejaculated my friend, not yet recovered from his astonishment.

"True," I replied; "the Amontillado."

As I said these words I busied myself among the pile of bones of which I have before spoken. Throwing them aside, I soon uncovered a quantity of building stone and mortar. With these materials and with the aid of my trowel, I began vigorously to wall up the entrance of the niche.

I had scarcely laid the first tier of my masonry when I discovered that the intoxication of Fortunato had in a great measure worn off. The earliest indication I had of this was a low moaning cry from the depth of the recess. It was NOT the cry of a drunken man. There was then a long and obstinate silence. I laid the second tier, and the third, and the fourth; and then I heard the furious vibrations of the chain. The noise lasted for several minutes, during which, that I might hearken to it with the more satisfaction, I ceased my labours and sat down upon the bones. When at last the clanking subsided, I resumed the trowel, and finished without interruption the fifth, the sixth, and the seventh tier. The wall was now nearly upon a level with my breast. I again paused, and holding the flambeaux over the mason-work, threw a few feeble rays upon the figure within.

A succession of loud and shrill screams, bursting suddenly from the throat of the chained form, seemed to thrust me violently back. For a brief moment I hesitated – I trembled. Unsheathing my rapier, I began to grope with it about the recess; but the thought of an instant reassured me. I placed my hand upon the solid fabric of the catacombs, and felt satisfied. I reapproached the wall. I replied to the yells of him who clamoured. I reechoed – I aided – I surpassed them in volume and in strength. I did this, and the clamourer grew still.

It was now midnight, and my task was drawing to a close. I had completed the eighth, the ninth, and the tenth tier. I had finished a portion of the last and the eleventh; there remained but a single stone to be fitted and plastered in. I struggled with its weight; I placed it partially in its destined position. But now there came from out the niche a low laugh that erected the hairs upon my head. It was succeeded by a sad voice, which I had difficulty in recognising as that of the noble Fortunato. The voice said –

"Ha! ha! ha! – he! he! – a very good joke indeed – an excellent jest. We will have many a rich laugh about it at the palazzo – he! he! he! – over our wine – he! he! he!"

"The Amontillado!" I said.

"He! he! he! – he! he! he! – yes, the Amontillado. But is it not getting late? Will not they be awaiting us at the palazzo, the Lady Fortunato and the rest? Let us be gone."

"Yes," I said "let us be gone."

"FOR THE LOVE OF GOD, MONTRESOR!"

"Yes," I said, "for the love of God!"

But to these words I hearkened in vain for a reply. I grew impatient. I called aloud –

"Fortunato!"

No answer. I called again –

"Fortunato!"

No answer still. I thrust a torch through the remaining aperture and let it fall within. There came forth in return only a jingling of the bells. My heart grew sick – on account of the dampness of the catacombs. I hastened to make an end of my labour. I forced the last stone into its position; I plastered it up. Against the new masonry I reerected the old rampart of bones. For the half of a century no mortal has disturbed them.

In pace requiescat!

PSYCHOANALYTIC CRITICISM AND 'THE CASK OF AMONTILLADO'

What's in a Name?

The names in Poe's story are over-determined – they have more value and meaning, more possible significations than a name would typically have. In normal discourse, a name is an arbitrary sign of a person's identity. On its own, it has no significance beyond standing in the place for a particular person. That my name is Andrew Slade bears no substantial connection, as a sign, to me. My name could be different and many parts about me would be the same. This is how names work in normal, everyday language. In certain ancient and premodern societies, the name of an individual differentiated him from others with the same name by reference to his parents or to his city. In the case of women, names are differentiated often in reference to her father and later her husband. In modern bureaucratic societies, there are other methods that are used to differentiate individuals with the same name – identity cards bear numbers, birth and death certificates record the date of birth as well as the city and parents' names. The name of an individual alone is not sufficient to guard against all kinds of mistakes of identity that can – and do – happen and which can have grave and devastating effects on people and communities. Yet, in telling stories with names, in normal and literary discourse, the name is often overdetermined or laden with meanings that as a name, in the strict sense, it simply does not have.

In the stories that we read and write, names acquire significance beyond that in normal discourse. In Poe's story, he offers us good European sounding names that signal, from an American perspective, the intrigues of a fallen European aristocracy. In postcolonial contexts, the names can signify the old structures of the colonial centre. Fortunato is literally 'the fortunate one' – that is what his name means. The fortunate one is the lucky one; he is the one character who, despite all that we do not know about him, will become the target of Montresor's envy and, ultimately, his act of revenge. The lucky one, Fortunato, ends up dying alone behind a masonry wall. The name Fortunato has another layer of significance by its intertextual reference to the Western literary image of the Wheel of Fortune. In the Western literary and cultural tradition, fortune was a kind of force in the world and was represented by a wheel. While one could be in good graces with fortune at one moment, the wheel could turn and one could go from the top of the wheel to the bottom with but half a turn. Fortune, while glorious when you have it, cannot be counted on. Fortune is fickle and inconstant. Poe's tale takes place in a very limited time frame and we do not see Fortunato's luck at the top of the wheel; but we see the murderous turn of the wheel. The name alone – through this analysis of the layers of association that we can link to this name – can allow us to see, in the core of the analysis, a fundamental part of the story. We have just used the methods of psychoanalysis to unweave one of the threads in Poe's text – the name Fortunato. There is nothing hidden in this reading – no meaning to uncover. Like the letter that Dupin finds clearly on the bureau in D___'s – the blackmailer – apartment, the significance of the name is out in the open when anyone can read it.

As a name, 'Montresor' is likewise overdetermined. While the tale takes place in Italy, Montresor is a French name – or better, it is a French phrase put together as a name. Montresor is, in French, 'my treasure'. The question that follows this name is obvious: What is your treasure? Reading Poe's text, there is no place where the first-person narrator calls himself Montresor. The narrator is called 'Montresor' by Fortunato. The narrator claims the name by claiming his family catacombs. Yet the story is narrated in the first person.

The narrator Montresor is clear about his intentions. The first paragraph of the story lays out those intentions and illustrates the mechanism of the ruse he plans to engage to seek his revenge. He invites the reader to collude with him and the irony of the text between Fortunato, Montresor and Poe's reader is shared only by Montresor and the reader. Fortunato is blind to his own fortune. Montresor sees what he is doing – he claims it as his own act and intention and he offers a theoretical justification of it. As he says, 'I must not only punish, but punish with impunity. A wrong is unredressed when retribution overtakes its redresser. It is equally unredressed when the avenger fails to make himself felt as such to him who has done the wrong.' Montresor will punish without getting caught in the punishment; and the one who is punished should know that he is the one doing the punishing. If anyone else were to find out about the punishment for the original wrong, that original wrong would persist. He does not name the wrong that Fortunato committed against him. He describes a difference between insult and injury, but he does not tell us what the injury is. That unnamed injury becomes the core that organises Montresor's overwhelming desire for retribution and revenge and, at the same time, he cannot name it. This is why, I would argue, that the name is significant in Poe's tale. Montresor is the name of the narrator given by the others in the tale – the reader, Fortunato and Poe. Just as Fortunato cannot recognise his own fortune, the narrator cannot recognise that element of his desire that drives his desire. He must have a treasure that Fortunato has harmed, but he will not begin to tell us what it is, his treasure, but it drives him to murder! The uncanny atmosphere and the drive to revenge are taken as given, without requirement of further explanation.

Freud talks about a kernel of a dream – that a dream has a basic core around which circulate the other dream images. Interpretation is the process that we undertake to unravel the significance in what appears insignificant. In the case of this story, there is an element of Montresor's desire that he cannot name or describe with any detail and which, nonetheless, drives his desire and the course of the narration. There is an element of the story that cannot become part of the story. This element of a story that cannot be rendered part of the story is what psychoanalytic theorists, who follow Lacan's teachings, call the 'real'. The real, according to Lacan, is what in a narrative is 'unsymbolisable'. The unsymbolised or unsymbolisable core of the story, of Montresor's story, is the unnamed injury. Montresor passes over it as if it were obvious – that the difference between insult and injury were so clear as to motivate – for anyone who would listen – the desire of a murderous revenge. His discourse is not deluded or paranoiac – he is not mad by any conventional representation of a madman in literature. He is cool and rational, calculated, deliberate and patient in his action. His name – his treasure – is that injury. It is precious – too precious to share.

The injury is a secret that must be kept secret. Only Montresor and Fortunato know the nature of the injury and so the retribution, according to Montresor's logic, must guarantee the secret of the secret. What is his treasure? His treasure is a secret. The names of these characters overdetermine the paths for meaning in the story – the reflection on these names and the pursuit of a literary and psychoanalytical methodology of close reading of the text and association on the manifest content, the text in its 'literality', in search of the latent thoughts. However, it is not enough to stop at either of these levels – of the literal or manifest content or the latent content of the story. Indeed, the names in Poe's story form part of a particular plot.

The Revenge Fantasy

Poe's story is a revenge tale. We do not know why Montresor seeks revenge on Fortunato, as we saw above, and we do not know what secret Montresor wants to keep or even if he knows that it is a secret that he is compelled to keep. The plot is the narrative mechanism that gives shape to the core of the fantasy – to get revenge for an injury. To seek revenge is a normal fantasy. Who has not suffered some kind of injury – no matter how slight – and entertained the idea of retribution? Perhaps, we have even carried out that retribution through more or less elaborate ruses or actions. The number and power of cultural responses to the threat of revenge indicates the power of the revenge fantasy. There is hardly an ethical, religious or cultural system that does not seek a way to discharge our desire for revenge by teaching and cultivating an ethic of reconciliation, forgiveness, renunciation of desire or acceptance. That people across cultures have sought mechanisms to constrain the desire for revenge indicates the power of the desire and its danger in the shared social and cultural world. Across cultures and histories, we have ways to understand the desire for revenge; at the same time, we have multiple remedies for that desire.

Writing a story of the desire for revenge is a way of transforming that desire. In 'Family Romances', Freud lists some basic injuries. We are injured in our ambition. For example, we might not achieve at a high enough level to get the social status that we wish we had. We may be jealous of someone else who gets what we want and whom we see as thwarting our ambition. We can be injured in our love object. In such a case, we are not loved and recognised as lovable by the one person we want to love us. This is the injury of rejection. In both cases, we perceive ourselves as injured for not getting what we want when we want it. This is an infantile structure that the unconscious, no matter how advanced we may be, refuses to yield. When we are injured, the ancient and primary mental response is to wish for revenge. Yet, we are not beholden to the infantile response alone. We struggle against it and the telling of the story of revenge is an effort in that struggle. Telling the story is not seeking revenge. Rather, telling the story is the sublimation of the drive that switches the aim from a sexual aim to a non-sexual one. The injury is put into the culturally valued work of art, in the case of the Poe story.

The plot, though, teases the reader along and allows us to enjoy Montresor's fantasy as if it were our own, in large measure because it is our own. Is there a man or woman who has not been injured in his/her ambition or in love? The appeal of the revenge story is to allow us to gain in fiction what we have denied ourselves in our lives. The appeal of the plot, of the time it takes the narrator to find Fortunato, to walk with him through the square during the carnival, to go down into the caverns in search of a rare and precious wine, and all of those elements of the plot and the plotting that in most of our lives we are restricted from pursuing, allow us to enjoy the process of revenge. In this sense, the story is an allegory of revenge that allows the reader who is in league with Poe, his narrator, and Fortunato, to enjoy what we would not admit to enjoying in conventional settings. In reality, we are not supposed to enjoy revenge. An insult that replays in the mind with the force of an obsession can become, through repetition, an injury – since an injury is an injury in as much as it is perceived as such. Montresor's unnamed injury begins as an insult. The plot moves us from insult, to injury, to revenge.

Setting or the Circumstances of the Plot

The story is set in Italy in carnival season. The carnival season is a season of ironic inversions. During carnival, normal social elements are suspended – the wise dress in the costume of fools. Fortunato wears 'motley'. The setting allows for the free play of the revenge fantasy that would normally be kept quiet or indulged in secretly. The carnival is an alibi for the open expression of repressed desires – such as the desire for revenge. It provides social and cultural support for anti-social wishes. As Freud describes in *Civilization and Its Discontents*, to live in civilisation – in organised society – the individual must renounce a certain amount and intensity of pleasure and satisfaction. The price of civilisation is satisfaction. The carnival allows for the open display of repressed wishes and desires and allows for their return within carefully circumscribed limits. The social context scaffolds, supports and frames the narrative elaboration of the revenge fantasy. If represented without the cover of the inversion of social rules into the carnival season, the revenge fantasy would be too much, too direct, too repulsive to lure all three players – Fortunato, Montresor and the reader – into the narrative to accept the fantasy. The context gives us all an alibi to enjoy our infantile fantasy.

The time in which Poe sets the narrative is only part of the story. The story's concrete setting, where most of the action takes place, is not above ground on the evening of the carnival. Rather, the narrator lures Fortunato deep into the damp and dark catacombs beneath the Montresor estate. The way into the catacombs is dark and damp. The walls are covered in nitre – a white mineral deposit of potassium nitrate or saltpetre. The catacombs are dark and the way to the cask of wine is long. The two men drink two bottles of wine on the way down; the ceiling is low. That the two men move down, deeper into the catacombs, suggests a cloacal journey. That is, the precious treasure, the cask of amontillado, is hoarded as a treasure. To hoard a treasure is an anal imagining. In the *Three Essays on the Theory of Sexuality*, Freud describes our infantile relationship to our faeces. Freud argues that faeces are associated with the possession of great value. His evidence for this is from his clinical experience and cultural interpretation. Money is often taboo – at once necessary but also dirty. But what is being hoarded? The catacombs do not appear to hold anything in particular that would provoke a remark either by the narrator or of Fortunato. We could venture that the Amontillado is there, of course. Yet, the wine never appears in the story except as a promise or a lure. The Amontillado gets Fortunato's attention and keeps him going down the catacombs. In the walk to the end of the catacomb where Fortunato is shackled to the wall and where the narrator, having shown his intentions earlier in flashing the trowel, seals Fortunato into the wall, we are left with the impression that the treasure that is being hoarded is the knowledge that Fortunato's injury has been redressed. Montresor's treasure is the walled-in Fortunato. Montresor preserves the limits of revenge in the terms that he has laid out in the first paragraph of the story.

The psychoanalytic reading of 'The Cask of Amontillado' engages the relationship between reader and text in order to produce a reading according to the terms that the text itself proposes. What can it mean to get revenge? This is the question that the text poses to the reader and which the reader traces through the plot of the story.

The plot is tied to the wish for revenge. The plot functions as what is openly visible, ready for anyone to read and access.

Poe's story is also an explication of the unconscious structure for the wish for revenge. Freud's texts return to the wish for revenge as a possible response to the experience of a wrong. What would be more natural, it seems, than for us to want revenge when we feel the pain of having been wronged! The wish for revenge is an infantile wish that can persist into adult life. In the case of this story, the unnamed harm that Fortunato commits against Montresor animates Montresor's desire for revenge. The time shelters Montresor's act. Indeed, the occasion of the carnival gives cover for Montresor's infantile desire and allows the reader to enjoy the fantasy as well – a fantasy that in waking life is too dangerous to admit. The reader, in following Montresor through to the end of his act, gets to enjoy what culture demands we not enjoy.

Why can we enjoy in writing what we cannot have in real life? Just as the dream eases the demands of the reality principle and the repression we live with in our cultures, the work of art – in this case, the story – allows us to enjoy what we cannot otherwise enjoy. In 'Creative Writers and Daydreaming' (1907), Freud approaches this problem from the perspective of the writer. The creative writer allows the wishes of his or her infantile life to enter the world of writing. Freud compares the work of the writer to the child at play (SE IX 143). The writer creates a world that is very much like the world of children playing: 'He [the creative writer] creates a world of phantasy [imagination] which he takes very seriously – that is, which he invests with large amounts of emotion – while separating it sharply from reality' (SE IX 144). The writer knows well that what happens in writing is not what she can have in reality. Reality demands a certain amount of renunciation; fantasy, or daydreaming, is a way to think about how the writer solves the problem of renunciation that culture demands.

The difference between the child and the writer is substantial. The child can resolve the demands of culture through play. The child's play can function without being impeded by others. Children do not conceal that they are playing even if they do not play in front of adults. 'The adult, on the contrary, is ashamed of his phantasies and hides them from other people. He cherishes his phantasies as his most intimate possessions, and as a rule he would rather confess his misdeed than tell anyone his phantasies' (SE IX 145). The writer wants his fantasies and nourishes them and then offers them to the public. The writer risks publicising his fantasies and so looks for alibis to distance his fantasies from himself. In Poe's story, the narrator attains that distance by setting the story in the carnival. What appears as an appeal to convention conceals a motivation for the display of the dangerous wish. The psychoanalytic critic sees the convention as the ruse that the author uses to allow the full expression of the forbidden wish.

In the story, however, we do not find the raw expression of wishes as we might hear them or read of them in clinical case studies. The works of art that the psychoanalytic critic analyses are examples of sublimation. Sublimation is the process of transforming sexual energy from a sexual to a non-sexual goal. Freud describes this process in detail in 'Instincts and Their Vicissitudes' in 1915. The classic examples of sublimation are artistic works and intellectual accomplishments. For Freud, sublimation is one of the possible diversions of libido or erotic energy. In sublimation, the sexual or erotic drive is diverted from its sexual goal and attains instead some other, socially valorised one. In the *Introductory Lectures on Psycho-Analysis*, Freud describes sublimation as a process that 'consists in the sexual trend abandoning its aim of obtaining a component or a reproductive pleasure and taking on another which is related genetically to the abandoned one but is itself no longer sexual but must be described as social' (SE XVI 345). In sublimation, the drive shifts its goal from a sexual one to a non-sexual one, or a socially valued goal. A writer writing turns the sexual drive into a socially valorised, social end. The psychoanalytic critic is then a reader of sublimations and also engaging in the process of sublimation. The writer's work, like a child's play, is a mechanism of attaining satisfactions that we are denied in reality. What we do not get directly, we can get through sublimation.

Sublimation, as we have discussed, is a process that brings the sexual drive to socially valued ends. Poe's tale of revenge, animated as it is by the wish for revenge, is given cover as a socially valued object – a short story. The story is not a report on actions; instead it allows the reader to enjoy the wish for revenge in the guise of a socially sanctioned activity. The intellectual activity of the psychoanalytic critic is the socially valued object that comes from a shift in the object of the drive. The pleasure of the revenge tale in Poe's story is the pleasure that comes from not doing what the tale represents. Psychoanalytic reading traces the surface of the text and interimplicates, through their mutual contact, text and reader. Psychoanalytic reading and psychoanalytic interpretations of literary texts should change our approach to the text and, in the best cases, our approach to what we believe about our own experience. As a clinical, literary anthropology, psychoanalytic theory and criticism links what is most human in us to the texts that we read and the stories that we tell.

Chapter Five

Psychoanalysis and Culture

One of the main criticisms of psychoanalysis has been that in its dogmatism of interpretation, cultural differences are erased in the name of conformity to established doctrine. In this chapter, we will look at one small section of psychoanalytic interpretation of an image from classical Greek mythology and other possible interpretations of the same kinds of images from different cultural perspectives. While the cultural perspective differs, the basic rhetorical and epistemological moves of psychoanalytic criticism remain. The image that we will look at is the hair of the Medusa. As we move along, we will come to understand the text as exemplary in the way it deals with culture and with gender.

'The Head of Medusa' (1595–96) by Michelangelo Merisi (or Amerighi) da Caravaggio*

*image courtesy: Wikimedia Commons

In Greek mythology, Medusa is a gorgon having the face of a woman and a tangle of snakes for hair. If you look at the gorgon, you will turn to stone. Freud wrote a brief note, 'Medusa's Head' (SE XVIII 273–74), in 1922, though it was not published until 1940. This short piece illustrates Freud's ability to leverage psychoanalysis in the interpretation of cultural symbols, but also shows the extent to which specific interpretations of images are grounded in the history and myths of cultures. Further, the short piece links psychoanalytic concepts and concerns quickly without substantial elaboration. While we might prefer a more subtle and nuanced style of interpretation – a style that we find in the best psychoanalytic writing – students can see some of the associations that have become predictable to those who are already in the know. The image of Medusa is also instructive because its interpretation, as Freud says, 'suggests itself easily' (SE XVIII 273). 'To decapitate = to castrate. The terror of Medusa is thus a terror of castration that is linked to the sight of something' (SE XVIII 273), Freud declares. As we have seen, castration is the condition of believing that we do not have what we most wish having. Castration anxiety is the life altering sense that we are incomplete and that we have already lost the primary object that would keep us most satisfied, that we have lost that total object that would quell all sense of dissatisfaction. In *The Interpretation of Dreams*, as we have seen, Freud indicates that this object is necessary though not actual – there is no such total object though that fact does not change our wishing that it were so.

Castration anxiety is the dread that reminds us – particularly boys and men – of this primordial loss. As the child develops, the sight of the mother's genitals, 'surrounded by hair' (273), can provoke intense anxiety. Freud situates that anxiety as the dread of castration that the child has hitherto repressed. The sight of the genitals allows the repressed material to return and, however momentarily, the belief in our own invulnerability is undone by what we seem to see. The sight of the genitals is not a dispassionate gaze or examination, rather the child's look, in spite of himself, is as of something that he should not be seeing but he is. That is the very definition of the return of the repressed that Freud gives in his essay on 'The Uncanny' (SE XVII). Repressed material often returns to consciousness in the visual field and this clinical reality allows the literary and cultural critic to interpret the visual images that abound in literature and culture according to this psychoanalytic insight.

Freud interprets Medusa's hair as the expression of material that he has gathered from his clinical work. Medusa, as is well known, has snakes for hair. Freud states clearly the dogmatic meaning of the snakes: 'however frightening they may be in themselves, they nevertheless serve as a mitigation of the horror, for they replace the penis, the absence of which is the cause of the horror' (273). What is horrible about Medusa is not the snakes, which in the West carry a strong association for fear and horror in their own right. Fear of snakes is common. Instead of provoking horror, the snakes mitigate or lessen the horror. How is this possible? A more conventional interpretation would suggest that compounding images of objects that normally provoke fear, like snakes, would naturally bring about more fear. Psychoanalytic interpretation is not satisfied with the manifest visual content; the replication of the number of the snakes compensates for the absence of the penis where it would be expected – from the genital area where it is absent, to the head where its stand-ins are multiplied. The replication of the penis images, the snakes, is an effort to ease anxiety. The replication of penis images is a 'confirmation of the technical rule according to which a multiplication of penis symbols signifies castration' (273). The replication of the penis substituted as snakes is a compensation and a reassurance for the threat of castration – look! There it is! It is not missing!

In the mythology of Medusa, she turns the one who sees her into stone. Freud notes that the response to seeing Medusa reproduces the effect of the castration complex, 'For becoming stiff means an erection. Thus in the original situation it offers consolation to the spectator: he is still in possession of a penis, and the stiffening reassures him of the fact' (273). Just as the sight of the many serpents that symbolise the penis reassures on the visual plane, the 'becoming stone' reassures at the level of the body.

The image of the Medusa is reproduced throughout Greek culture on the dress of Goddess Athena. Athena was represented with an image of the Gorgon's head on her dress. The mythology of

Medusa is not limited to the particular stories of a minor character in the lives of the gods and goddesses, but is dispersed across the entire pantheon of the gods, by this fact of representation.

Athena is represented as a fascinating but unapproachable woman. She is a representation of a woman who 'frightens because she is castrated' (274). Freud's method is to find in the mythological story those elements of an anthropology that illustrates the ways in which humans negotiate their struggle in the social world with their internal pressures.

The text on Medusa is a fragmentary one and is more suggestive than exhaustive. At the same time, the text points to a potential link between the symbols of classical psychoanalysis and the symbols that are used by individuals from different cultures at different historical moments to render their experiences meaningful. In the social and cultural history of representations of the Medusa, Freud sees an opening for a research programme: 'In order seriously to validate this interpretation it would be necessary to investigate the origin of this isolated symbol of horror in Greek mythology as well as parallels to it in other mythologies' (274). Bound as he is by the limits of his moment in modernity, Freud seeks validation through finding 'parallels' with others rather than with, as more current anthropology would insist, allowing other symbolic systems to exist in their own right. Yet, his gesture suggests the possibility of a culturally bound psychoanalytic interpretation of cultural symbols. In such a programme, psychoanalytic ideas about the importance and power of symbols can be brought to bear on a variety of local practices. In this sense, psychoanalysis is not necessarily a universalising and totalising discourse that denies all cultural difference. Rather, psychoanalysis, in this light, is open to a full range of historical, national and cultural expressions.

In his book, *Medusa's Hair*, the Sri Lankan anthropologist and psychoanalyst Gananath Obeyesekere brings the mythology of Medusa and her hair into dialogue with cultural and religious symbols of certain 'religious virtuosos' (Obeyesekere 1), mainly Hindu ascetics, from his fieldwork in South Asia. The first part of Obeyesekere's book treats the symbol of matted hair. His primary concern is how personal experience is related to cultural meaning (13) and he situates the work between two inadequate perspectives. An anthropological perspective that treats matted hair as if it were simply the expression of cultural practices is as inadequate as an account of the practice that would consider only the psychological meaning of the symbol. The symbol cannot be only cultural or only psychological. His work addresses the intersections of culture and psyche. In this, Obeyesekere is very much in the tradition that Freud's programme suggests, though the latter was not able to carry it out. He concludes, 'The complex personal experiences of the individual are crystallized in the (public) symbol. Thus symbols like matted hair operate on the psychological and cultural levels simultaneously; ergo, a naïve psychoanalytic position is as inadequate as a naïve anthropological one' (13). Freud's sketch of the meaning of Medusa's hair, I would argue, is a naïve psychoanalytic one in Obeyesekere's sense even though it opens the space for a sophisticated research trajectory that would link the cultural and the psychological values of the symbol – matted hair.

Obeyesekere contributes to the expansion of anthropological and psychoanalytic knowledge through the link of the private psychological symbol with the public cultural one: 'Personal symbols must be related to the live experience of the individual and the larger institutional context in which they are embedded' (13). In its dogmatic or naïve posture, psychoanalysts and psychoanalytic critics sometimes forget that they need to pay attention to the fine grains of the analysand's discourse, to the discourse of the text. Indeed, the psychoanalytic critic ought to pay careful attention to the articulations of the text and to the public world where those articulations find their meaning. In this sense, I would argue with Obeyesekere, that psychoanalytic criticism and theory must be attuned to the cultural determinations of discourse and to the private experience that the texts circulate around. This is what I have tried to show in the analysis of Edgar Allan Poe's story, 'The Cask of Amontillado'.

I have pointed to Freud's text on Medusa as an instructive, if limited, approach to linking personal and cultural symbols. A certain strand of dogmatic psychoanalysis, quoted and critiqued by Obeyesekere, elevates Freud's remarks to the level of established truth. In a book by Charles Berg, *The Unconscious Significance of Hair* (1951), hair is equated to the penis and therefore cutting the hair is equivalent to castration. The argument is similar to Freud's observations in the text on Medusa. Of course, Freud does not stop with the dogmatic claim and signals the need for further elaboration and research. Obeyesekere provides some of this research, though it is moved from the Western context of Greek antiquity to the ascetic practices of South Asia. He incorporates psychoanalytic insight, the insistence on the value of personal symbols, into the broader project of anthropology and its effort to understand the cultural, public symbols that scaffold personal symbols. In fact, personal symbols cannot be merely personal any more than they can be merely cultural. What does Obeyesekere find?

First, Obeyesekere interviewed women ascetics of Sri Lanka. He presents his interviews in the style of case studies, providing significant background and specific details of the personal experiences of his informants. The interviews took place over a considerable time so as to allow him to speak to the informants in their 'own idiom and experiences' (22). His study focuses on three female ascetics and the cultural and personal symbolism surrounding their matted hair. The two naïve approaches outlined above form the backdrop or intellectual context of his interpretive strategy.

Obeyesekere analyses the meaning of the symbols from three points of view. First, he analyses the 'origin and genesis of the symbol' (33). Where does the symbol come from? Second, he analyses the personal meaning of the symbol for each ascetic. What does the person say the matted hair means to them? Part of his analysis must include the public meaning of the symbol and so he analyses the meaning of the symbol for the group. What does the matted hair mean to the communities in which the ascetic lives? Third, what social and cultural messages does the symbol 'communicate to the group' (33)? Psychological analysis, he argues, is most important at the first level of interpretation, because the symbols adopted by his ascetics tend to be linked to experiences that are 'painful, complicated, and out of the reach of conscious awareness that the individual must express them with indirect representations' (33).

Individuals may express painful experiences in ways that exceed their conscious control over them. He does not argue that the symbol is a symptom in a psychoanalytic sense, though there is another thought that occurs. The symbol may be a way in which an individual works through a painful experience to integrate that experience into the rest of his or her life.

The psychoanalytic concept of working through is helpful to understand this process by which, as Obeyesekere states, the symbol of the matted hair is '*recreated* each time by individuals' (33, emphasis added). The individual adopts a public symbol but recreates it each time that she adopts it. It is not a repetition of an extant symbol, but a recreation of the symbol as if it were altogether new. In the process of the recreation of these symbols, he notes three processes. First, there is the 'loss of sexual love' (33). Second, the ascetic idealises a divine lover and detaches from the actual husband. The divine becomes an idealised father and husband (33). Third, the ascetic renounces eros and embraces agape. She rejects carnal love and takes on the detached love of the divine. In the Greek tradition, eros is linked with the body and sexuality. Erotic love is a love in which the lover seeks to be filled in with the love of the beloved. Agapeic love is a love that flows from divine abundance and overwhelms the lover in its plenitude. In eros, the lover is a vessel that can be filled with the beloved, while in agape the lover is swept away by the overwhelming power of the beloved's love for her. Eros is almost always sexual, while agape is almost always chaste. In the case of the ascetics, the 'god's gift for having renounced eros for agape is matted hair' (33). The matted hair is a gift that does not signify castration but its opposite – plenitude or blessing.

As in Freud's analysis of the Medusa, the symbol of the penis emerges on the head. Freud's Medusa is first the castration anxiety of the male projected onto the female figure and associated with the female genitals. Castration anxiety is related to the absence of the penis. In the case of Obeyesekere's ascetics, we have access to the subjective and historical experience of women with matted hair and not just the mythological and cultural symbols of it. Freud's analysis focuses on the social, cultural and mythological meaning of the Medusa rather than the genesis of the meaning of the symbol.

For the ascetic, the matted hair is a gift for having renounced the erotic penis for the divine penis of the god. The matted hair of the ascetic is a sign of commitment to the god and a rejection of the human penis. In Freud's text, the Medusa is the externalisation of castration anxiety and its projection onto the body of the woman. The woman reminds the man of what he fears he may lose.

The experience of Obeyesekere's ascetics, indeed, the perspective that his project adopts, differs from Freud's speculative remarks. Freud cannot hear the voice of the Medusa, indeed, she has no voice in Freud's text, only a terrifying visual appearance. Obeyesekere's essay opens to us the voices and experiences of women with matted hair and inscribes them into the cultural and historical location that allows their voices to speak meaningfully about their experience. Obeyesekere does not reject the psychoanalytic model of interpretation on the basis of his informants. Instead, he keeps the method and adjusts the content of his interpretations to better account for the narratives of his informants. In this way, his approach to the Medusa and the image of the matted hair avoids the reductionism of any dogmatic approach to psychoanalytic interpretation and allows for the words of the informants (or the analysands) to be heard on their own terms.

Obeyeskere's approach to the image of the matted hair as a psychological and cultural symbol can be a model for literary and cultural critics to follow, in particular as regards texts and objects that are not obviously included in the mainstream of the Western traditions that Freud assumed. Freud's assumptions need not be our realities. As we have seen in the reading of Poe's text, there are explicit strategies for psychoanalytic critics to read that do not demand that we acquiesce in the assumptions of the West. Obeyeskere's anthropological arguments push us further still to see that it is possible to understand a range of cultural expressions with psychoanalytic structures guiding interpretations of locally-inscribed signs.

Conclusion

The purpose of this book has been to offer students of literary and cultural studies an avenue for entry into psychoanalytic criticism and theory. The method has been to focus on the core elements and texts of Freud's thought. What remains for the student to do – what remains for the student now – is what always remains for all students. What remains is to read. If the book has been successful, it will suggest some lines of inquiry beyond the introduction. It will suggest some models to follow that draw together the strengths of psychoanalysis and literary criticism. These disciplines, though they have distinct aims, share elements of methodology. Psychoanalysis is a discipline founded in listening to the stories and the thoughts of others. In order for Freud to develop any of the claims that I have described here, he had to first listen to others who were suffering. He listened to learn, but also to help. His clinical work was oriented towards the cure. He believed that psychoanalysis would cure if it were correctly done.

Literary criticism shares the concern of the text as primary. Without engaging in a history of theory and criticism, I will assert that literary criticism, regardless of the theoretical commitments of the writer, begins with an effort to listen to the text. And, psychoanalytically, to listen to the text means to listen to, read, what the text says before one reads for meaning. I have tried to demonstrate this act in the brief chapter on 'The Cask of Amontillado'. Like psychoanalysis, literary criticism is an intersubjective act; and writing literary criticism in a psychoanalytic way is a testimony to that intersubjective situation and it bears witness, or it ought to bear witness, to the effects of that interaction. As the chapter on the Medusa suggests, the risk of psychoanalytic criticism is dogmatism. I would hope that the book shows a way to engage with psychoanalysis that is loyal to Freud and what has come since Freud in psychoanalytic thinking and, at the same time, avoids the dogmatism that turns the analyst into a master who cannot be challenged.

What remains for psychoanalytic criticism and theory is open, of course, as any future must be, to the possibility that what has happened may return. That we may have to answer again, perhaps differently, perhaps not, the riddles that continue to appear in human experience and which psychoanalysis addresses and which literature dramatises. Psychoanalysis developed with literary examples and models. Without literature, it would be hard to imagine psychoanalysis. What I suggest, after a century of psychoanalysis and after it has established itself all over the globe, is that literature now needs psychoanalysis too.

My hope is that this book opens up psychoanalysis for you and will be useful in helping you to venture further into Freud's writings, further into your own readings of literary and cultural texts, further into your own programmes of research and application. The psychoanalytic study of literature, I am convinced, will yield further insights into how we live together well and where our problems lie, to suggest a way to understand those problems as particularly human problems. Psychoanalysis is an anthropological discipline that addresses vital human questions in much the same way that literature is a vital human passion and a place where we tell ourselves and others what and who we think we are. In this, psychoanalysis and literature belong together.

A Brief Glossary of Psychoanalytic Terms

Students of psychoanalysis will find many dictionaries of psychoanalytical terms that have been published through the years. The purpose of this glossary is to permit the student to gain quick and ready access to key terms in psychoanalytic thought – in particular, to Freud's lexicon. The entries are not exhaustive. For a dictionary of psychoanalytic terms that aims to be exhaustive in its coverage, please refer to *The Language of Psychoanalysis* by Jean Laplanche and Jean-Bertrand Pontalis.

Anal: The second phase of the organisations of sexuality that Freud described, this phase is characterised by the act of withholding an object and expelling it. The model for the behaviour is learning to control the bowels.

Condensation: One of the mechanisms of the dreamwork. In condensation, multiple dream thoughts are represented by one object or image.

Displacement: One of the mechanisms of the dreamwork. In displacement, one dream thought is represented by another, usually a less affectively dangerous dream image.

Dream: The basic mechanism through which the unconscious can satisfy its wishes; other mechanisms include sublimation, symptoms and slips of the tongue or pen.

Ego: In the later, dynamic conception of the mind, it is the location of conscious thought and action, though it retains what in earlier formulations, Freud discussed in terms of the preconscious mental functions. The Freudian Ego is not the same as the ego of Enlightenment philosophy.

Fantasy: One of the modes of fulfilling a wish in which the subject maintains a degree of agency or autonomy over the content of the wish

Genital sexuality: The unified version of sexuality where the components of sexuality – oral, anal and others – are combined and unified in normal adult sexuality. According Freud, genital sexuality is oriented towards reproduction.

Id: In the later, dynamic conception of the mind, the Id is Freud's name for the unconscious as a dynamic, wishing process.

Oral: The first phase of sexuality described by Freud, the oral phase is characterised by sucking and is related to nourishment and takes as its objects, the breast and the mouth.

Overdetermination: Dream images signify more than they suggest in regular discourse; as contorted dream thoughts (through the processes of condensation or displacement) the dream image always has a surplus of significance. Its significance can suggest multiple, often competing or contradictory, meanings.

Masochism: Associated with the anal phase of sexual development, masochistic impulses find pleasure in making the ego the object of abuses.

Perversion: in a clinical sense, it is an abnormal sexual relation with a partial object that derails the normal aim of sexuality. In perversion, a part of the body is taken as the sexual aim in the place of the genitals.

Pleasure principle: Principle of mental functioning that aims to regulate human, mental excitation at a constant level with neither too much nor too little stimulus. In *The Interpretation of Dreams*, it is characterised along side a principle of constancy. The point is to keep us at a level of homeostasis relative to pleasure and unpleasure. It was also referred to as the 'unpleasure principle', but later pleasure principle was Freud's preferred formulation.

Psychosis: Mental state characterised by the dissolution of the difference between the ego and the other; it is characterised by delusions and hallucinations.

Reality principle: The fact of the external world and its demands impresses upon the unconscious restrictions to the access to satisfaction. The reality principle is externalised through the demands of civilisation and internalised through the education of children through the phases of sexual development.

Repression: Defense mechanism whereby unconscious ideas that are felt to be too dangerous to become conscious are, by a secondary force, pushed out of consciousness but which can be brought into consciousness in certain circumstances

Sadism: Associated with the anal phase of sexual organisation, sadistic impulses take pleasure in harming beloved objects.

Sexuality: It is the broad lines of development over the human lifespan. Freud believed that sexuality is more fundamental to human mental life than the specific behaviours of adult sexual practice. Consequently, sexuality and its various forms (oral, anal, genital) underpin all human mental life.

Sublimation: Sublimation is one of the possible paths that a drive can take on its way to satisfaction. Standard examples of sublimation include intellectual or artistic work as in these activities, the sexual drive is diverted from its sexual aim to a non-sexual one that is highly valued culturally.

Super-ego: In Freud's later, dynamic conception of the mind, the super-ego is the locus of repression and guilt as the agency of the moral law and the will of the 'father'.

Transference: In the intersubjective analytic situation, transference emerges in the attribution of desire or thought or feeling to the other, regardless of whether the attributed desire or thought actually belongs to the other.

Uncanny: It is the sense of dread that comes about when one encounters something that is familiar, yet somehow strange at the same time. Freud describes the uncanny with reference to E. T. A. Hoffman's tale, 'The Sandman'. In Freud's reading of that tale, the uncanny is linked to a sense of dread when something that should remain hidden from our conscious life becomes suddenly, strangely conscious.

Unconscious: The unconscious is the primary process of mental life, according to Freud.

Wish fulfilment: In the theory of dreams, the unconscious seeks to have its wishes fulfilled and uses dreams to attain its satisfaction.

Bibliography and Texts for Further Reading

Ahktar, Salman, ed. *Freud Along the Ganges: Psychoanalytic Reflections on the People and Culture of India*. New York: Other Press, 2005. Print.

Atikal, Ilanko. *The Cilappatikaram of Ilanko Atikal*. Trans. R. Parthasarathy. New York: Columbia UP, 1993. Print.

Bonaparte, Marie. *The Life and Works of Edgar Allan Poe: A Psychoanalytic Interpretation*. New York: Prometheus Books, 1980. Print.

Breton, André. *Manifestoes of Surrealism*. Trans. Richard Seaver and Helen R. Lane. Ann Arbor Paperback, 1972. Print.

Felman, Shoshana. *Jacques Lacan and the Adventure of Insight: Psychoanalysis in Contemporary Culture*. Cambridge, MA and London: Harvard UP, 1987. Print.

Fink, Bruce. *Clinical Introduction to Lacanian Psychoanalysis: Theory and Practice*. Cambridge and London: Harvard UP, 1997. Print.

———. *Fundamentals of Psychoanalytic Technique: A Lacanian Approach for Practitioners*. New York and London: W. W. Norton, 2007. Print.

———. *The Lacanian Subject: Between Language and Jouissance*. Princeton: Princeton UP, 1995. Print.

Freud, Sigmund.

[All references from, Strachey, James, gen. ed. *The Standard Edition of the Complete Psychological Works of Sigmund Freud* [SE]. 24 vols. London: Hogarth Press, 1994. Print.]

———. 'A Childhood Recollection from *Dichtung und Wahrheit.*' SE XVII, 145–56. Print.

———. 'Creative Writers and Daydreaming.' SE IX, 141–53. Print.

———. *Delusions and Dreams in Jensen's Gradiva.* SE IX, 3–95. Print.

———. 'Family Romances.' SE IX, 235–41. Print.

———. *The Interpretation of Dreams*. SE IV–V. Print.

———. 'Medusa's Head.' SE XVIII, 273–74. Print.
———. 'The Uncanny.' SE XVII, 217–56. Print.
———. *Leonardo Da Vinci and a Memory of His Childhood*. SE XI, 59–137. Print.
———. 'Wild Psychoanalysis.' SE XI, 219–27. Print.

Geyskens, Tomas. *Our Original Scenes: Freud's Theory of Sexuality*. Figures of the Unconscious 6. Leuven: Leuven UP, 2005. Print.
Geyskens, Tomas and Philippe Van Haute. *Confusion of Tongues: The Primacy of Sexuality in Freud, Ferenczi, and Laplanche*. New York: Other Press, 2004. Print.
———. *From Death Instinct to Attachment Theory: The Primacy of the Child in Freud, Klein, and Hermann*. New York: Other Press, 2007. Print.
International Psychoanalytic Association. https://www.ipa.org.uk.
Jahanbegloo, Ramin. *Indian Analysed: Sudhir Kakar in Conversation with Ramin Jahanbegloo*. New Delhi: Oxford UP, 2009. Print.
Kahn, Michael. *Basic Freud: Psychoanalytic Thought for the Twenty-first Century*. New York: Basic Books, 2002. Print.
Kakar, Sudhir. *Culture and Psyche: Selected Essays*. London: Oxford UP, 2008. Print.
Lacan, Jacques. *Ecrits: The First Complete Edition in English*. Trans. Bruce Fink. New York and London: Norton, 2006. Print.
Laplanche, Jean and Pontalis, Jean-Bertrand, eds. *The Language of Psychoanalysis*. New York and London: W. W. Norton, 1974. Print.
Obeyesekere, Gananath. *Medusa's Hair: An Essay on Personal Symbols and Religious Experience*. Chicago and London: U of Chicago P, 1981. Print.
Vaidyanathan, T. G. and Jeffrey John Kripal, eds. *Vishnu on Freud's Desk: A Reader in Psychoanalysis and Hinduism*. London and Delhi: Oxford UP, 1999. Print.
Verhaeghe, Paul. *New Studies of Old Villains: A Radical Reconsideration of the Oedipus Complex*. New York: Other Press, 2009. Print.
———. *On Being Normal and Other Disorders: A Manual for Clinical Psychodiagnostics*. Trans. Sigi Jottkandt. New York: Other Press, 2004.

Literary Contexts recognises that literature is always rooted in its social milieu and that we need to study literary cultures in all their complexity and connections. It offers the thrill of locating a text within its context and seeing a context reflected in a literary/cultural text.

Each of the books in the series offers students of English and other literatures concise, informative insights into the history of ideas embodied in literary texts, authors and movements. Organised around themes and ideas with extensive examples from literary and cultural texts, the books enable students to understand how the "literary" takes shape in an intellectual milieu and discover manifestations of abstract ideas in literary texts. Written by scholar-teachers who have taught and researched literature for several years, each volume in the series is a stand-alone reference book for students and teachers alike.

Series Editor

Pramod K. Nayar teaches at the Department of English, The University of Hyderabad. His most recent books include *The Transnational in English Literature: Shakespeare to the Modern* (2015), *Citizenship and Identity in the Age of Surveillance* (2015), *The Postcolonial Studies Dictionary* (2015) and *Postcolonial Studies: An Anthology* (2015). His forthcoming work includes a book on the Indian graphic novel.

Titles in the Series

Shakespeare
American Literature
Modern English Literature
Eighteenth-century English Literature
Postcolonial Literatures
Victorian Literature
Postmodern Literatures
English Romantic Literature